To: Clint,
my esteemed
colleague &
"Brother" in the
common academic
enterprise!

O LORD, MOVE THIS MOUNTAIN

God's
blessings!

--Enoch

O LORD, MOVE THIS MOUNTAIN

RACISM & CHRISTIAN ETHICS

E. HAMMOND OGLESBY

Cover Design: Elaine Young
Art direction: Michael Domínguez
Interior design: Elizabeth Wright

This book is printed on acid-free, recycled paper.

Visit Chalice Press on the World Wide Web at
www.chalicepress.com

10 9 8 7 6 5 4 3 2 1   98 99 00 01 02 03

Library of Congress Cataloging-in Publication Data

Pending

Table of Contents

Foreword

Enoch Hammond Oglesby has written a seasoned, reflective book on the demands and expectations of Christian ethics with reference to the intransigent challenge of racism. It is time for a reflective analysis after the shock waves of social protest and the emergence of liberationist categories of interpretation. Oglesby supplies that need in a first-rate fashion, because a number of important perspectives converge in his study in a most suggestive way.

Oglesby works the metaphor of "mountain" effectively, by which he refers to racism that, like a mountain, sits in the middle of our life as an ominous presence as a latent threat, complex, an obstacle blocking our common way, and yet waiting to be overcome. Clearly Oglesby has thought long and struggled in concrete ways with the issues, to the great benefit of those who read him.

The book is a consequence of long, careful work on the major literature of Christian ethics, with particular attention to Reinhold Niebuhr, Paul Lehmann, and Walter Rauschenbusch. Along with these major figures, he makes helpful reference to Jim Wallis and Peter Paris. What surprises one most is appeal to Martin Buber; perhaps Oglesby is most in tune with Buber in his conviction that reconciliation can come only through dialogue, or as Buber might say, through "meeting."

The book is deeply rooted in the faith and life of the church; Oglesby writes as a Christian theologian and a serious believer. He understands that the overcoming of racism is not a cerebral matter, but finally concerns the concrete practice of serious people who care. Indeed, he has shaped his book for practice, as he provides not only case studies but reflective questions as well, that will aid in moving from thought to concrete act.

The book is the testimony of an African American who has lived with and through heavy doses of the indignity and suffering of racism that I suppose is nowhere to be avoided in our diseased society. Oglesby is reflective and candid enough to bear witness to the hurt and rage that linger for him. The tone and intent and strategy of the book are indeed conciliatory, but he knows very well that reconciliation must engage in no deception—of self or of other—but must be an exercise in truth. Thus the story he tells bears the deep marks of particularity and contextuality. The reader is invited to a process of discernment of the pain and promise of the black religious experience in America—an experience not fully contaminated by affluent individualism.

All of these aspects of Oglesby's thinking—disciplined Christian ethics, sturdy church faith, and lived African American experience converge in the theological pivot point of "covenant-harambee." The hyphenated term of course appeals to the communal binding of the faith in the Old Testament. The second term bespeaks a solidarity and togetherness in suffering and joy that is the seedbed of human newness. By such a focus Oglesby clearly invites us to an image and a practice of a very different humanness, a humanness rooted in God's gift that offers us all freedom from the savage mountain.

I was privileged to be Oglesby's teaching colleague for nearly two decades. During that time I regularly conversed with him and was instructed by him; no doubt I taught him patience (!) as I sought to come to terms with my own habitation in "the mountain." It is a delight now to commend this book that reflects his most mature thinking. It is an instruction to us all.

Walter Brueggemann
Columbia Theological Seminary
May 29, 1997

Preface

We Wear the Mask

We wear the mask that grins and lies,
It hides our cheeks and shades our eyes,—
This debt we pay to human guile;
With torn and bleeding hearts we smile,
And mouth with myriad subtleties.

Why should the world be over-wise,
In counting all our tears and sighs?
Nay, let them only see us, while
    We wear the mask.

We smile, but, O great Christ, our cries
To thee from tortured souls arise.
We sing, but oh the clay is vile
Beneath our feet, and long the mile;
But let the world dream otherwise,
    We wear the mask!
                    —Paul Laurence Dunbar, 1872–1906

Every day people from all walks of life—whether they are African Americans or other people of color—seem to be forced by circumstances: fortune or folly, rage or righteous indignation, character or courage, to simply "wear the mask." As an African American theologian I think that the colorful ritual of *mask-wearing* has been elevated to a Shakespearean art form in many quarters of the black middle class community, in the Promethean attempt on the part of many to crash through the "glass ceiling" of achievement in white America. In the rhythmic flux of moral struggle for equal justice and dignity, many people with a shared memory of oppression and hope still find it difficult to cross boundaries—of religion, denomination, age, sex, nationality, culture, social class—and instead, quietly accommodate themselves to the genteel art of *mask-wearing*. In a culture constantly dripping with ambiguity and rage, living always at the intersection of hope and despair, there is wisdom in the observation that people often wear the mask for complex reasons. For some folks, the art of wearing the mask is a way of suppressing a xenophobic memory of the wrongful deeds of chattel slavery that continue to haunt blacks today; for others in the Anglo-European community, it may be a failure of will or conscience to simply correct racial injustices and wrongdoings inherent in the American social system by those who hold strong positions of power and responsibility. Perhaps for the masses of us, however, the burden of wearing the mask emanates from the basic impulse to survive, the terrible contradictions and calamities of human existence. Whether it is born out of cowardice or the impulse of survivalism, there is, I think, a deep spiritual moral price that we as Christians pay for wearing the mask that calmly "grins and smiles" on the outside of the human self, while the inside remains a raging river.

Whenever theologians, writers, and leaders of the church tell stories they are often asked: "Did that really happen? Is the story really true? Are the events in the story reasonably trustworthy?" Well, in the cases and stories that appear in this book, I can answer with a resounding "YES!" They are true and can be trusted; only the names of the characters in the stories, for the most part, have been altered. For example, I vividly recall a chilling story shortly after my arrival in St. Louis, Missouri, as professor of Christian social ethics at Eden Theological Seminary back in 1978. The incident involved an invitation I had received from a local white pastor to come and speak on something like "global peace and prayer" or "Race Relations" Sunday at his church. We shall call this pastor "Harold." In the desire to do things "decently and in order," this benevolent invitation was given to me at least a year in advance. As a frequent speaker and lecturer in many middle class white congregations of St. Louis, I eagerly awaited the opportunity. Since, after all, Harold was the son of one of my colleagues in Christian ministry. I was also told at that time that a black man had never preached from this "white" pulpit. This factor alone created a fluttering edge of anxiety in my soul, but not beyond what I am usually accustomed to in dealing with interracial congregational settings. Theologically and perhaps naively, I reasoned to myself: "After all, we're all just God's people; red, yellow, black or white, we're all precious in God's sight!" Well, as things turned out, it wasn't necessarily "God's sight" that proved disturbingly normative in this situation, but the "sight" of white church folks! The result of this true story is that about three weeks prior to the occasion, I was sadly told by the minister that the invitation had been withdrawn—while on my way to lecture, ironically, in my class at Eden on the topic "Ethics and church life." "They don't think they are ready yet for a black man to preach from their pulpit," said the young white pastor. Naturally, I was taken aback by this incident and judged it to be a very "unchristian" thing to do, especially in a theological community steeped in a rich ecumenical heritage and tradition of German liberal Protestantism and Evangelical piety. Yet this rich tapestry of ethnic diversity among European immigrants that came over from Europe in the 1840s to the frontiers of the Midwest did not easily co-mingle—either culturally or religiously—with the sons and daughters of African slaves. Be that as it may, I remember only that in the surprise of that moment, I felt wounded, angered, hurt, and betrayed by this liberal white pastor of St. Louis.

Notwithstanding, I wore a "mask" of avoidance, silence, and estrangement from Harold for approximately fifteen years as we would, inevitably, see each other at public gatherings and seminary conferences. Interracially, what was a molehill became a mountain. What was once genuine fellowship turned into the shame of alienation, as a quiet storm of rage replaced the nurturing bonds of Christian *koinonia* deep within my soul because I had been wounded by the decision to withdraw the invitation to speak at Harold's church. Of course, for me, it wasn't the speaking *per se*, but the whole moral principle of what is right and wrong. Ethically, I judged that behavior to be morally wrong and racially offensive. But the point in this little story I wish you would see is simply this: the burden of the ethical for forgiveness and reconciliation between Harold and me was as much *mine* as *his*. Why? Because I wore the tamed "mask" of

avoidance and rage for fifteen years, which no human being necessarily should feel compelled to wear or bear; because the delicate
web of life itself is too precarious. Since life is partial to irony and
surprise, I recently met Harold again at a public gathering at Eden
Seminary in 1995, and I broke the "ice" and we became reconciled.
Maybe in a rare solitary act of forgiveness, it is possible to get a *vision
beyond the mountain*. In any case, sometimes the undue burdens of
racism can result in wearing the mask too long. Now in our current
reflections in this book on the dialectics of moral struggle, ministry,
and ethnic relations we shall attempt to *unmask* and to better understand the phenomenon of racism in American life. Accordingly, this
study will explore certain metaphors and shades of meaning and
will provide an honest ethical attempt to get at socio-historical and
foundational expressions of racism in both church and society. What,
then, constitutes a viable ethical method which by definition or
discourse sheds light on the ethical-thing-to-do in the cruel face of
racial bigotry? Can the church make a difference as we wrestle with
the demonic "stranger" within and without, or is the church now
part of the problem in contemporary society? Logically, we may ask:
"What is the purpose of the case?" The case method itself helps the
moral agent to explore and keenly examine one's own values, beliefs, cultural traditions, and experiences as possible gifts to be lifted
up and celebrated. In any event, the "case" offers an angle of vision
and an invitation to cross-cultural dialogue that may open up new
vistas of learning and self-understanding among women and men
of faith—with exceedingly complex histories of oppression and hope.

In addition, we shall explore the particular story or case of
"Grandma Ella" as a vehicle for understanding certain ministry issues that many people face—as they arise from the diverse experiences of real people, confronting real problems in a multicultural
and multiracial society. Unfortunately, there are no simple answers
to complex issues of the head and heart, where the agonizing search
for a viable ethical method to the meaning of human existence on
the part of the moral agent is ceaseless. In the contemporary field of
Christian social ethics, scholars and leaders in the church seem to
accommodate their methods to the needs, interests, demands, and
hopes of a confused and fragmented society. Concretely speaking,

the ethicists and theologians that I know and respect in the field refuse to use "cookie-cutter" or "one-size-fits-all" approaches. Like many of my colleagues, I agonize over the question of "ethical method" or the appropriate use of theological language that can unpack the thorny issues and moral dilemmas of "multiculturalism and diversity" in ministry as we confront the future, hopefully, with the liberating power of the gospel of Jesus Christ.

Accordingly, what I shall attempt to do in this book is to offer, in part, a modest proposal in our discussion, which I refer to as a *covenant-harambee* method of ethical discourse. Now the perennial vision inherent in this ethical approach is, as I see it, both invitational and confessional. What it attempts to critically proclaim, and remind us in the life of the congregation, is this: "Don't let the world squeeze you into its mold, but let God's righteousness and liberating love re-mold you and us, as one emerging body in Jesus Christ!" Therefore, I contend, passionately, that the language of this ethical approach or method affirms the dialectical tensions of both love and justice, of hospitality and hostility, of freedom and responsibility, and of suffering and hope as ordinary people work at the difficult task of establishing moral boundaries for decision-making and action in an increasingly chaotic world, where racism is still alive and well. In white America, for instance, the scapegoating of black people, Jews, Latinos, Asians, Native Americans, and others is a very old game. Biblically, the prophetic viewpoint demands that the old game of "unrighteousness" stop and the new game of "righteousness" start. At every juncture of ethnic relations in America, the struggle for justice requires a new start, a new spirit of seeking and striving." "Strive first for the kingdom of God and his righteousness, and all these things will be given to you as well" (Mt. 6:33).

1

The Racism Dilemma and the Church

The judgment of God is upon the church. The church has a schism in its soul...It will be one of the tragedies of Christian history if future historians record that...the church was one of the greatest bulwarks of white supremacy.

—Martin Luther King, Jr.

When I was growing up in the years of the high-water marks of the civil rights movement, the church was a dynamic symbol of the *soul* of the community, the citadel of divine praise and promise, the house of culture and character formation, and the web of protection for young children and elders against the brutalizing forces of racism and oppression in a hostile world. It was in the nurturing womb of the church where the web of protection first wove its indelible lines across the character of my being, as a young African American male growing up in the cotton-belt township of Earle, in northeastern Arkansas. Indeed, it was here at the St. James Missionary Baptist Church where the web of protection was most deeply felt in the cradle of my being—as Rev. J. L. Davis, my hometown

1

pastor, preached constantly, like a scratchy needle on a broken record, from a variation of the same biblical theme: "the power and paradox of God's suffering love for sinners and oppressors." Of course, my home was experienced as a "web of protection" also—indeed, it was the first. But the church itself was the social playground for all the neighborhood kids. It was something *more*; this innate feeling of something *more* seemingly permeated the climate of the neighborhood and gave order and civility to our social world.

Looking back, it was here in the church where the web of protection, both spiritually and metaphorically, established for me internal boundaries of self-esteem against the external forces of racial bigotry and moral degradation, experienced by so many young black children at the hands of the wider society. Concretely speaking, if "race" was the perennial burden on the backs of black folk in America, the church of my community helped to ease the weight of that burden. For example, my childhood friend and classmate Charles Robinson, at a recent class reunion (1996) of the Dunbar High School of Earle, Arkansas, mused to the gathering: .

> My friends, looking back at our beloved Dunbar—we had good teachers, but hand-me-down textbooks from the public schools; we had good basketball players, but no gym to practice in…remember, our players had to travel five miles to the neighboring town of Parkin, to practice at the "Colored" high school…because Earle High (white) barred us from their gym…we had good preachers back then, in our own churches and community, but they couldn't preach Bible from white pulpits…things today "done-changed-some," but I'm still outrageously mad about that….

The reality of the phrase "done-changed-some" that fell from the lips of Charles Robinson points us to the moral dilemma and paradox of the state of ethnic relations in contemporary American society. This brief leaf from the notebook of my high school class reunion is an important window from which to see the racism dilemma and the church today. On the eve of the twenty-first century, I am warmly struck by the fact that in the community of Earle, my old classmate Charles made history and became the first black superintendent to head this formerly segregated public school system, a bastion of genteel Southern culture and racial bigotry. That is the good news; I identify with and joyfully celebrate these precious and often rare moments of ethnic progress among blacks and whites. In retrospect, the bad news is that Rev. J. L. Davis, my childhood pastor whom the larger black community loved and respected, could never preach the same liberating gospel of Jesus Christ—though using the same Bible as our fellow white Christians—from any white pulpit of the South. The bad news is that the church across the tracks—i.e., the white church—functioned as a protector of, and sanction for, the prevailing cultural values and racist practices of a segregated social order. To be sure, the "symbolic 11 o'clock worship hour" in the church on Sunday morning was the most segregated hour in America. It is no wonder, in the ethics and theology of Dr. King, that the church in context of North American society was largely viewed as "one of the greatest bulwarks of white supremacy." Hence, the racism dilemma that one sees in the educational, political, and economic institutions of the wider society is a mere microcosm of a *huge mountain* in our time.

The Quest for Metaphors: A Mountain?

Add up bootstraps, ballots, bucks, and the need for visionary clarity on the complex question of racism, and what do you have? With any cursory glance, I submit that we have a mess! I would further say: "There ain't no easy way out of the mess we're in; so a sinking, messy situation calls for new imagery." The current institutional images of racism stink! For example, consider the tired and worn-out metaphors such as "pulling yourself up by your own bootstraps," "black and white together," "we've come a long way, but got a long way to go," or try this one on for size: "I don't see color; I only see people as just people!" It seems to me that the emerging composite from all these divergent images demands a new metaphor: a mountain. I suspect that the above images or icons are tired not just because those images derived their life blood from the "successes" of the old civil rights movement but also because Christian ministry on the eve of the twenty-first century *is in a new place.*

Analytically, mountains as a term have no standard geological meaning. They generally refer to a land form that rises well above their surrounding area and have steep slopes. Generally, the summit of a given mountain is confined.

Mountains are rarely found as a single peak. More often, they are found in belts or chains which, when linked together, form a mountain range. These ranges are then jointed to form a mountain system. Most ranges in the world are connected to the Circum-Pacific System and the Alpine-Himalayan (or Tethyan) System.

Moreover, we may say that mountains are formed by the collision between lithospheric plates that form the earth's outer shell. The collision causes folding, faulting, or upwarping of the earth's surface. It is thought that the formation of mountains is a relatively recent geological process. Erosion is believed to be able to level mountains if given enough time.

Another manner in which some mountains have been formed is the result of subduction. This is "...the sinking of one plate beneath another at convergent plate boundaries," according to *Encyclopedia Britannica*. At the leading edge of these plates a portion of the lithospheric layer is melted by contact with the asthenospheric layer (the layer of molten rock below the lithospheric layer). Consequently, the melted rock is expelled as lava and pyroclasts at the surface. Steep volcanic cones dominate such areas.

The major mountain types include dome, fault-block, fold, and volcanic. Again according to the *Encyclopedia Britannica* (1993 edition), "Dome mountains are produced by fractureless upwarping of the surface. They have a comparatively flat, dissected surface that gradually slopes toward the adjacent lowlands" (p. 376). Fault-block mountains are made up of portions of the earth's crust that have been thrust upward along linear fracture zones in the form of enormous blocks. "Fold mountains are formed by lateral compression and attendant uplift. They tend to occur where extensive basins have been filled with layers of sedimentary rock material. The cover of stratified, unmetamorphosed sedimentary rock reacts differently from the underlying basement rock of granite or gneiss when subjected to compressive forces." Moreover, simple-fold mountains come into being when "...the sedimentary rock cover is folded by sliding laterally over the basement" (p. 376).

Volcanic mountains "...occur near subduction zones and with fault zones that are attendant on major orogenic activity" (p. 376). There are two types of volcanic mountains. One is a direct result of volcanism. The second is the result of the residual products of volcanism. Now the upshot of this brief treatise on the nature and types of mountains is to underscore the importance of a common imagery in the physical world as a "social metaphor" for racism in today's society. If the faith we confess is to be alive in the works of interracial justice, then the reality of the mountain (racism), as social metaphor, must be clearly understood by all people of goodwill—whether they be Anglo-Christians, Latinos, Native Americans, African Americans, Asians, or other people who walk upon the earth.

The Uneven Landscape of Racism

I believe passionately and contend that for some people the church in our time—either by neglect of the gospel of Jesus Christ for the poor and oppressed, or by compromise of God's unrelenting righteousness and truth—has come to symbolize the "grand mountain" of racism in American culture. As I see it, the deep tragedy of the church today is in its compromise of *faithfulness* to the biblical mandates of justice, love, mercy, mutuality, and the affirmation of the equality of all persons as children of God. The church's blatant compromise of the ethical teachings of Jesus on matters of race, sex, class, ethnicity, and cultural inclusivity—to name just a few—has led to what I call the grand mountain of racism in our society. Joseph Barndt, in his cogently relevant book *Dismantling Racism: The Continuing Challenge to White America*, hits the nail on the head concerning the compromise of the church to the demonic force of racial bigotry. He writes:

> Not only have the church's teachings been compromised, but the church itself has become a part of the prison of racism, its leadership co-opted into assisting the warden and the guards. The historical fact is that the church has often blessed deliberate acts of direct racism. The church, together with other institutions in contemporary society, remains captive to the continued systemic racism of the present and is to a great extent still unrepentant for it.[1]

---

[1] Cf. Joseph Barndt, *Dismantling Racism: The Continuing Challenge to White America* (Minneapolis: Augsburg Fortress, 1991). This volume makes an important contribution to our critical understanding of racism in the context of white America.

It is hard for us to come to grips with the fact that the *racism dilemma* strikes at the very core of white culture and theology, which tends to put most Christians in a difficult position of compromise among many mainline churches in American society.[2] The deadly seed of racism is sown deep into the soil of American culture—with its destructive root system invading and distorting our collective memories and national myths, hopes and dreams, and our rituals and customs that should function to give a person or group a sense of coherence and order in human life. Racism breaks the order of social existence. For us as moral agents, racism violates the normative rule of rational coherence by the failure to recognize its own irrationality in human society. For us as Christians, racism distorts the ethical teachings of Jesus Christ through the sins of omission and commission. By *omission*, I mean to suggest that the predominantly white church in the United States does not generally lead its members to *confess* the sin of racial bigotry. Here the act of confession, in the context of Sunday morning worship, for instance, typically excludes any reference to racial bigotry. To borrow a phrase from Jim Wallis, editor of the magazine *Sojourner*, racism is "America's original sin."

As an African American professor at a predominantly white theological institution, I know firsthand the pain and frustration that often accompany the scandalous reality implicit in the liturgical omission of the "sin of racism." While I am keenly aware of the capacity of liturgical language to "name" and express many realities, let me illustrate a part of the racism dilemma by citing a "typical" prayer of confession. This is how one white seminarian, leading worship, inadvertently expressed it:

> God, we set before you the needs of a world which is torn and divided. We are all members of your one human family, yet we stand against each other and do not speak words of peace. You have made us one in the spirit whose bond is peace, yet we stand unconcerned though peace is not yet real. Forgive us the wounds we have caused and the wounds we have refused to notice. May what we do here be our task in life and one sign of hope for people. So may we give you fitting praise on earth today and every day. Amen.[3]

[2]Ibid., pp. 123—130.
[3]*Worship Service of Word and Sacrament*, "A Prayer of Confession" (St. Louis, Missouri: Eden Chapel, October 1993).

I am not suggesting here that the legitimate guardians of church life and liturgy are necessarily indifferent to the problem of "race" or intentionally vicious on the question of racism as a "sin of omission," but rather that many appear to be blatantly insensitive and ignorant when it comes to people of color, and *how* we "confess," and *what* we confess as a praising–giving people to the God of biblical faith. By *commission*, I mean to suggest to the reader the various ways by which the church has historically aligned itself with the prevailing cultural values, attitudes, rituals, and customs of the middle class vis-à-vis the poor and marginalized ones in our world.

Because of the seductive powers of individualism and greed in the contemporary society, the church has become a "prisoner" of an individualistic middle class orientation, the chief defender of the prevailing values of the status quo. By appealing to cultural expediency *over* God's reign of righteousness for the poor and oppressed, the church has accommodated the wrong gospel, and acquiesced to a racist social order. In the classic work *The Social Sources of Denominationalism*, H. Richard Niebuhr speaks boldly on how the church has, largely, sold its soul to the gods of "middle class religion."[4] It is only a glimpse into the obvious to see how this ethico-theological problem contributes to the racism dilemma in mainline Protestant churches in the United States. In light of the view of racism as a sin of *commission*, one call also see the class bias of a Eurocentric Christianity and the relevant critique of Niebuhr's theology. For example, the church makes this point nicely. He asserts:

> Middle class religion…is not only distinguished from the faith of the poor but also from the Christianity of the landed gentry and their…dependents…Hence the religion of the bourgeoisie seeks separate organization not only on account of the economic conflicts of the class with aristocracy above and the proletariat below but also because of the divergent religious attitudes and desires which arise out of these class differences.[5]

---

[4] H. Richard Niebuhr, *The Social Sources of Denominationalism* (New York: Henry Holt and Co., Inc., 1929), pp. 85–94.
[5] Ibid., pp. 88–89.

It is profoundly significant to observe, therefore, the manner in which the class differences further aggravate the racism dilemma among mainline Protestant churches in America. Thus, black folk are faced, in this regard, with a double-barreled moral dilemma: the sinful scandal of racism within the comfortable pews of the church, on the one hand; and, on the other, the immorality of bourgeois power arising from the church's uncritical identification with the dominant class values of the status quo. This unholy union of both "class" and "race" accounts for the gradual process by which the basic "prophetic claims" of biblical faith were radically compromised by the church to the developing interests of a rising bourgeois culture in Europe as well as in North America.[6]

Thus the reality of "class differences," according to Niebuhr—with its affinity grounded in the Calvinist conception of individual rights and responsibilities—personified the conflictual virtues of *laissez-faire* capitalism and liberal pietism, and perhaps pushed further to the margins of history the biblical imperative to "do justice," in regard to the oppressed and hurting ones in our world. For cultural and ethnic relations in the church universal, it seems to me that the biblical imperative has always been crystal clear. For example, the prophet boldly sets forth the ethical dictum:

> He has told you, O mortal, what is good; and what does the
> LORD require of you but to do justice, and to love kindness,
> and to walk humbly with your God? (Micah 6:8)

Is the Church Guilty of Racism?

Notwithstanding, it is apparent, in my opinion, that most Eurocentric scholars, theologians and teachers of the church never really seem to get the point of the biblical imperative of linking it to the problem of the "racism dilemma" in our dominant religious and sociocultural system. Put another way, the religious leaders and defenders of "middle class religion" literally dropped the ball when it came to the ethical application of the biblical imperative to matters of ethnicity and religio-cultural diversity in the body of Christ. Generally, people of color have been historically excluded from full

---
[6]Ibid., pp. 88–89.

participation in mainline white Protestant churches in white America. The profound gravity of the "racism dilemma" in the contemporary church is keenly illustrated in the provocative work *The Soul of Politics*, by Jim Wallis.[7] By contrast, Jim Wallis candidly speaks of his dramatic eye-opening experience with African American Christians, along the road of his own pilgrimage into the pain and eschatological promise of black life in the United States. Recalling fragments of this cross-cultural encounter, he writes:

> I started by seeking out black churches. As I asked my question a whole new picture of the world began to emerge. Black Christians made time in their very busy lives for a young white kid who was full of questions…They were extraordinarily patient and receptive, never patronizing…They must have been smiling inside at my questions, which had such obvious answers, but they never let on. My pilgrimage into the black community opened up a whole new world and would affect the rest of my life.

> The simple, self-justifying worldview of my childhood and my church, in conflict with my growing awareness of racism and poverty, caused mounting havoc in my teenage years. I was shocked at what I saw, heard, and read; I felt betrayed and angry by the brutal facts of racism. Worse, I felt painfully implicated.[8]

It seems to me that this frank and compelling testimony by Jim Wallis is a rare ethical moment of genuine confession dealing with the historical dialectics of the pain, racial bigotry and hope— expressed by one brave soul who seized the opportunity for cross-

[7]See Jim Wallis, *The Soul of Politics: A Practical and Prophetic Vision for Change* (Maryknoll, New York: Orbis Books, 1994). As a prophetic voice in the interest of poor and oppressed peoples in this land, Wallis writes with passion and imagination about his vision for a better world, and the critical issues at stake in order for us to achieve a better world, reflective of God's suffering love and the hope for a new community. "With this hope, we can look into the eyes of the poor, the suffering…and believe that God is able to establish justice for all. With this hope, we can together build a new community," says Wallis, "that will some day overcome the barriers of race and class and gender" (p. 240).

[8]Ibid, p. 76.

cultural interaction and dialogue. Vividly recalling his early involvement and encounter with blacks—especial manual laborers and unskilled workers in the "motor city" of Detroit—Wallis suggests that the black religious community was nothing less than a street corner laboratory of "new education." "The young blacks I met were much more angry and militant than the black Christians I had come to know," says Wallis, "and they provided me with a new education."[9] I suspect that the upshot of this case scenario from Wallis' book *The Soul of Politics* underscores an important angle of vision on the "racism dilemma" in contemporary society, namely: History teaches us that black Christians in the dominant host culture have, apparently, appropriated the essential moral teachings of the Christian message in such a way that allows for more openness and acceptance of whites in the "House of the Lord" than the reverse.

Furthermore, I contend that certain lessons of history reinforce this critical point as we continue to grapple with the racism dilemma in both church and society. Rethinking the racism dilemma also demands a keen sense of history and awareness of ethnic relations in our democratic republic. William Wells Brown, the noted nineteenth-century novelist and historian, reminds us that "we are what we remember." To be sure, the relevance of historical understanding sheds light on the problem of racism in the contemporary society, without which the Christian message of love, justice, and reconciliation loses its vitality. Thus in the Troeltschian spirit of ethical discourse, the morally sensitive person finds it imperative to make historical comparisons in order to convince the reader or hearer of the seriousness of racism in regard to the dialectics of ethnicity and ecclesiology. I am convinced, therefore, that the situation of racism in America critically demands an alternative historical perspective.

An Alternative Historical Look

Comparatively considered, Peter Paris, in his critically acclaimed volume *The Social Teaching of the Black Churches* articulates the argument that black folks found creative ways to deal with the "racism dilemma" in the post-antebellum world of Jim Crowism and ecclesial

---

[9]Ibid., p. 76.

segregation in the white churches.[10] The so-called "creative ways" refers to the selective manner in which black folk were able to discern nonracist forms of the Christian message mediated through the dominant ecclesiological structures of modern Protestant thought. Now reflecting, historically, on the development of black churches in America, Peter Paris boldly asserts:

> In the white churches not only had blacks perceived a deliberate distortion of the Christian gospel but they feared a loss of their own self-respect should they continue indefinitely in a proscribed form of association with whites. From slavery through the period of Reconstruction they resolved to find ways of separating themselves from the religious and moral corruption endemic in the white churches in order to gain a measure of independence wherein they might affirm their own humanity in the light of a nonracist appropriation of the Christian message. Thus racism functioned as a negative cause for the separate racial churches, while blacks themselves constituted the positive thrust for independence.[11]

It is ironic that while the "slippery mountain" of racism contributed negatively to the formation and development of racially separate churches in America, black Christians themselves were able to turn a "negative" into a *positive*, by struggling against the smothering blanket of fear, hatred, and violence at the hands of white rulers. Indeed, it is hard to imagine how these ragtag black Christians, fresh out of the labor fields of chattel slavery, could not only build institutions capable of surviving in a hostile environment but also construct a moral worldview of their own that did not exclude the real *humanity* of white folks. As I see it, this is one of the most profound and startling cross-cultural achievements within the annals of ethnic history and faith in the modern world. Theologically, we are driven to ponder reflectively, these questions: What sort of moral tenacity enables the individual to "bless" the ones who "curse" you? To affirm and include the basic humanity of those who

---

[10] Peter J. Paris, *The Social Teaching of the Black Churches* (Philadelphia: Fortress Press, 1985), pp. 3–10.
[11] Ibid., p. 6.

exclude and scornfully dehumanize you? What manner of people seem to find within their hearts the impulse to practice forgiveness over wrongdoing, love over hate? Indeed, what manner of people out of Africa found the collective will to embrace an alien culture in the United States, whose Eurocentric ancestors regarded black people as inferior and subhuman? Put sharply, what can change or Christianize the hearts of those who found it, apparently, so easy to subordinate and brutalize black folks in the United States?

Now part of the answer, I think, to these perplexing questions stems from an alternative moral view of the world, which blacks embraced, a moral view deeply rooted in biblical faith and in the crosscurrents of African culture and religion. The irony of this alternative view, implicit in black church life and achievement, is captured by Paris when he writes:

> Those nascent black churches evidenced the cooperative action of slaves to build institutions and prove to themselves and others that they were capable not only of adapting to an environment but of constructing a world of their own....While the larger society sought to victimize blacks, the black churches aimed at socializing their members into creative forms of coping along with the development of imaginative styles of social and political protest, both grounded in a religious hope for an eschatological victory.[12]

In making the case against the problem of racism in both church and society, in regard to the need for an alternative perspective, Peter Paris sharpens the historical focus. He rightly articulates the heart of the issue in which white Christians are implicated:

> Contrary to the general opinion among blacks, white America experienced no dilemma between its theological thought and the way it treated blacks. For white America it was not a matter of believing in true justice while practicing injustice. Rather, in that respect, the white churches actually experienced no alienation between their thought and practice. This is evidenced by the fact that any attempt to preach racial equality

---

[12]Ibid., p. 6.

in the pulpits of white churches has always been viewed as an act of hostility against their prevailing ethos.[13]

Seeing the Mountain Darkly: Alternate Definitions of Racism

Racism, like many other terms in ethnic literature and folk culture, is not an easy term to define because theologians and social scientists define it in many ways, and in the process, they often use the *same terms* to mean different things. Thus some critical comparative analysis is useful at this point. To begin with, *What is racism?* We need to be aware of the confusion and of the often conflicting interpretations surrounding the question of definition, *per se*.

From a conceptual framework, let us now consider several alternate definitions of the racism dilemma in both church and society. From the outset of our reflections, we may simply turn to the dictionary. According to the *Random House Dictionary of the English Language* (1967), racism is "(1) a belief that human races have distinctive characteristics that determine their respective cultures, usually involving the idea that one's own race is superior and has the right to rule others; (2) a policy enforcing such asserted rights; (3) a system of government and society based upon it."

Through the initial definition of racism one can see the so-called "distinctive characteristics" expressed by one individual or group which may lead to the subordination of another individual or ethnic group. It is well for us to point out that the particular elements of the "will-to-power" and the "will-to-be," implicit in the above definition, pose a menacing dilemma in ethnic relations today. Another definition of racism may serve to illuminate the social situation. Describing both personal and institutional forms of racism, the United Church of Christ, in its *Pastoral Letter on Contemporary Racism and the Role of the Church*, issued this cogently relevant statement:

> Racism is both overt and covert. It takes two, related forms: individual whites acting against individual blacks, and acts by the total white community against the black community. We call these individual racism and institutional racism. The first consists of overt acts by individuals, which cause death, injury

[13]Ibid., p. 76.

or the violent destruction of property. This type can be reached by television cameras; it can frequently be observed in the process of commission. The second type is less overt, far more subtle, less identifiable in terms of specific individuals committing the acts. But it is no less destructive of human life. The second type originates in the operation of established and respected forms in the society, and thus receives far less public condemnation than the first type.[14]

Probing further on the question of "definition" into the corpus of our sociocultural studies, the reader may observe the following view expressed by Joel Kovel in his perceptive work *White Racism: A Psycho-history*. He argues:

> If racism has had a stabilizing effect in our culture and helped sustain its "higher" elements by binding up the "lower,"...then our culture is markedly less virtuous than ideology would have it. Our ideals are nourished by corrupt roots and survive by a continuously sustained act of self-deception.[15]

Theoretically, a careful look at the problem of racism here enables us to see it—analytically—as a difficult cultural phenomenon which cannot be fully understood outside the cultural milieu. By probing further, the phenomenon of racism transcends particular institutions—either ecclesiological or educational—and lodges itself within the attitudes and folkways of the dominant Eurocentric culture. It seems to me that it is here where the demonic force of racial bigotry can best exploit, separate, deceive, and further alienate suffering humanity into the camps of the "haves and the have-nots."

---

[14]See *Pastoral Letter on Contemporary Racism and the Role of the Church* (Cleveland: UCC Commission for Racial Justice, UCC, 1991), pp. 12–13.

[15]Joel Kovel, *White Racism: A Psychohistory* (New York: Vintage Books, 1971), p. 4. Perhaps what is most fascinating about this particular story of racism is the careful analysis given to the shaping forces of history, and how they bear upon our values, sentiments, and hopes in the American sociocultural system. Hence, showing what is intriguing about this long historical development of ethnic relations and social struggle, Kovel underscores the irrationality, perverted symbolism, and cultural banality of racism in the whole of Western culture. Accordingly, Kovel argues: "Symbols and fantasies of racism have been themselves generated by the history of race relations and sustained by the rest of an organically related culture" (p. 7).

Our persistent struggle for educational awareness and faithfulness to the church must remind us of the "divide-and-conquer" mentality so pervasive in the racist ideology. Ingrained deeply in the web of Western culture, *racism is like a rattlesnake: and rattlesnakes don't commit suicide!*

For example, the National Education Association issued an informative publication entitled *Education and Racism:An Action Manual.* The framers of the document offered certain pragmatic guidelines in the attempt to increase educational awareness about racism in the United States and beyond. It clearly says that racism in the United States is *primarily* a white problem. Crucial for both religious and secular communities, the critical insights are here stated:

1. Third World histories and cultures are not usually presented with honesty in our educational processes, but rather are portrayed from a white ethnocentric viewpoint (e. g., the term *minority groups* is used in spite of the reality that *whites* are in the minority internationally).

2. White racism exists because of the power historically possessed by whites, which has enabled them to exercise the control necessary to dominate the institutions and cultures of our society. The following conditions are necessary for a racist society:

   (a) Oppressed should usually feel psychologically and culturally inferior.

   (b) Oppressors should usually feel superior.

   (c) All citizens should accept the cultural standards of the oppressors.

   (d) Oppressors should usually fear the oppressed.

   (e) Oppressors should usually show the ability to practice genocide against the oppressed (Albert Memmi).

3. White racism is not an independent factor but is interrelated with all aspects of our society and most particularly with the political and economic sectors.

4. White racism is operative not only internally in the United States, but also in our international relationships, resulting in the exploitation of all Third World peoples.[16]

---

[16]See *Education and Racism: An Action Manual* (Washington, D.C.: A National Education Association Publication, 1973) pp. 25–35.

Again, comparatively speaking, we should return and consider the working definition of racism—implicitly and explicitly—explored in Joseph Barndt's volume, *Dismantling Racism: The Challenge to White America*. He argues, and I think rightly so, that racism goes beyond mere prejudice. Any person or member of a given ethnic group can, in fact, be prejudiced. "Prejudice" means pre-judgment which leads to "mis-judgment"—whether that person be Euro-American, Asian, Latino, Native American, or African American—just to name a few. But the phenomenon of racism, according to Barndt, is by definition radically different. For Barndt, "Racism is prejudice plus power." He argues for the distinction in this manner:

> Everyone is prejudiced, but not everyone is racist. To be prejudiced means to have opinions without knowing the facts .... to be racially prejudiced means to have distorted opinions about people of other races. Racism goes beyond prejudice. It is backed up by power. Racism is the power to enforce one's prejudices.....(p. 28)[17]

In terms of perennial reflection and analysis of the wider problem of racism in America, let us now consider the following diagram that may shed further light on this perplexing moral dilemma in our time:

---

[17]Joseph Barndt, *Dismantling Racism*, p. 28.

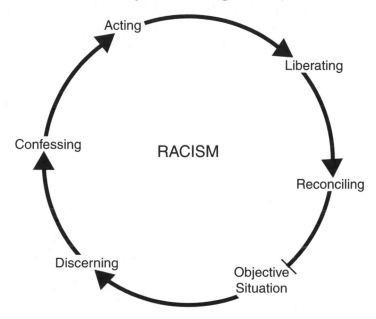

SOCIAL DIAGRAM:
Racism Cycle—Breaking the Pattern

Acting
Liberating
Confessing   RACISM
Reconciling
Discerning   Objective Situation

Orientational Aspects

An interpretive analysis that is genuinely theological can be illustrated in what we call the "Racism Cycle." This cycle represents the close relationships between six mediations of experience: (1) acknowledging the *Objective Situation* of racism in American society which cannot be easily ignored by ethically sensitive Christians in the life and faith of the church; (2) the act of *Discerning* means a willingness to "name" the reality of racism to acknowledge how we as social selves participate in it, and derive benefit from it— given the complex social system which tends to disproportionately reward white people for being "white" and, by the same token, to victimize people of color for being "colored"; (3) the cycle itself requires that the moral agent engage in the faithful task of *Confessing* to the reality of racism as being "America's Original Sin," to borrow a phrase from Jim Wallis, a noted activist for peace and justice; (4) it is my ethical stance that each Christian in church and community has a moral obligation not only to "confess," but to participate in the creative process of *Acting* on behalf of the Holy One of Israel who has called us out of the darkness of racial prejudice and fear into the marvelous light of Christ's love and newness ("So if anyone is in Christ, there is a new creation: everything old has passed away; see, everything has become new!" 2 Cor. 5:17); (5) the "Racism Cycle" can only be broken as the bigoted person or the marginalized one struggles to be open to the *Liberating* presence of God as revealed in Jesus Christ. In the rhythmic flux of biblical history it is this same compassionate God who can break the yoke of systemic oppression in high places of power and greed; it is this same compassionate God who can cut loose black stammering tongues from the inner prison of fear and the outer prison of white male domination and Western economic imperialism; it is this same compassionate God who can liberate the hurting ones from the self-destructive webs that exist on the mountain of racism; undoubtedly, it is because of God's liberating presence already manifested in Jesus Christ that the Christian community has hope in the struggle to overcome the mountain of racism in the United States. Moreover, I wish to suggest that a viable orientational diagram on the problem of racism or other "isms" must include the organic principle of *reconciliation;* (6) in human community. Here it seems to me that the mediation of the experience of God's *Reconciling* love has the power to reunite the separated and alienated ones: the oppressed and the oppressor, the haves and the have-nots, the marginalized and the landed gentry, the learned and the unlearned—that all may come to know as *we are known* by the one Transcendent Spirit. In sum, the "Racism Cycle" invites us to genuine dialogue in human community about the things that matter.

Now, considering the complexity of theoretical definitions on the question of racism, it seems clear to us that each—given this cursory glance—sheds light on our current moral dilemma in the wider society. Each definition of racism, in the various contexts, I suspect, is necessary but not sufficient. While I can say, as an African American Christian ethicist, with some passion that only whites can be racist in the United States, because of their position of domination and control of the economic, social, and political institutions—that knee-jerk analysis alone is not enough. I am painfully aware, as a follower of Jesus Christ, that the capacity to hate can take many forms of cruelty, like the horrible deeds of the Holocaust against Jews—but only those who have power can enforce the legions of hate and human annihilation. While I can see the rage of prejudice and violence simmering in the "dark ghettos" of urban America, I am painfully aware that it was white America—through the arrogance of power, greed, and moral neglect—that actually created the awful conditions of the black ghetto. While I may simply *know* about the terrible conditions of exploitation and injustice experienced by blacks and other Third World peoples around what Robert McAfee Brown calls our fragile "global village"—I lament the fact that the same marginalized people do not have access to power to either enforce their will for the good of the oppressed or the destruction of the oppressors. So then, by definition, people of color in America cannot be *racist*.[18] Racism equals racial prejudice plus power. This observation is not based on some self-righteous ethnocentric understanding of anthropology which proclaims, "People of color are, by *nature*, better than people from Euro-American ancestry!" I suspect that such an anthropological claim would be false; and it would be the epitome of cultural arrogance, which denies our common humanity as children of God (*imago dei*). Rather what I mean to suggest by the assertion "Blacks in the United States can't be racist" is the glaring empirical fact that African Americans do not have the *power* to impose their will on the "majority" group in the dominant culture. Perhaps now we have come to the heart of the matter on this question of racism in the body politic of both church and society. Because we recognize the power of racism to humiliate and destroy blacks and other people of color, it is my fundamental thesis that an alternative definition is needed to the more generalized theories on racial prejudice and ethnicity implicit in the corpus of social science.

Here the language of "metaphor" is a useful tool in regard to the phenomenon of racism. For example, the term metaphor is derived from the Latin word *metaphora*, which literally means "to carry

---

[18]Cf. *Education and Racism: An Action Manual*, p. 12.

over, transfer, or move beyond." Moreover, the notion of metaphor is a critical figure of speech that denotes one kind of idea is used in place of another by way of suggesting a likeness between them. Metaphorically considered, therefore, it is the basic thesis of this book that white racism in America is a treacherous and slippery mountain that we all must attempt to climb in order to avoid the increasingly corrosive demise of democracy, the cultural imperialism, and the galloping moral and spiritual bankruptcy of the church. Existentially, I am convinced, in the deep river of my soul, that if we—for whatever reason—do not choose to engage in battle to climb the "mountain," all our hopes and dreams for our children and for a better society marked by justice, equality, mutuality, and compassion will be lost. It can be argued historically, for instance, that the reality of racism-as-mountain was captured in this prophetic line from the black leader James Weldon Johnson, who once remarked: "The race question involves the saving of black America's body and white America's soul."[19] Here let us take a closer look at the metaphor.

Racism Is a Mountain

It is more than a glimpse into the obvious to suggest that the reality of racism decrees a set of loyalties and energies that either empower us to climb the *mountain* or pacify us sufficiently to be satisfied with the "strange fruit" from the fields at the base of the mountain itself. Whether the *mountain* appears to be good or evil, right or wrong, moral or immoral, tasteful or distasteful—all depends on one's cultural location, status, skin color, eccesial loyalties, values, and position in the socioeconomic system of American society. While the vested interests of Euro-American Christians and people of color do, in fact, vary—given the wide range of goals, opportunities, and pressures from our societal institutions—the one constant refrain that cannot be avoided is the mountain of racism itself.

Theologically discerned, God did not authorize the church of Jesus Christ to merely set up camp at the foot of the mountain of

---

[19]Cited in Barry N. Schwartz and Robert Disch, *White Racism: Its History, Pathology and Practice* (New York: Dell, 1970), pp. 1–2.

racism in America but rather to climb the mountain itself: to struggle and suffer together, to conquer and move *beyond* America's "original sin." The tenacity of moral witness against the mountainous evil of racism is, I think, the primordial challenge of Christian ministry in today's complex world of multiculturalism and theological diversity.

For instance, the experience of racism as a treacherous mountain on the part of black people in America continues to shape our collective vision, self-understanding, and theological construction. Accordingly, Gayraud Wilmore has asserted: "Black theology, explicating the faith that Jesus Christ came to liberate the captive masses of the world, has played a crucial role in unmasking the racial sin of Western Christianity...the ideology of white supremacy."[20] Thus we can see more clearly that the mountainous evil of racism is linked dialectically to the biblical imperative to seek justice in the face of racial injustice and to affirm the cruciality of moral struggle for liberation over the demonic forces of cultural imperialism and ethnic oppression.

Existentially, I shall toil and never quit—as I am faced with the mountain of racism in the United States—until I climb this mountain. In the wisdom of the black church tradition, I proclaim, in the liberating name of Jesus Christ, and unto the freeing and unfailing God of our weary years and silent tears, that this *mountain must go*! In the rhetorical voice of the black preacher, I shout poetically to heaven above:

Give Us This Mountain!

O mountain, be thou removed,
like scrapes of lead paint that
kill our children in the
projects of the dark ghetto;

O mountain, be thou removed,
like lethal gas that quietly
and unknowingly rocks me into a slow sleep of
death, in my middle class suburban enclave.

---

[20]Cited in George C. L. Cummings' *A Common Journey: Black Theology (USA) and Latin American Liberation Theology* (Maryknoll: Orbis Books, 1993), p. 35.

O mountain, be thou removed,
like the powerful winds of Heaven,
that gently splits the earth; purifying and
separating the East from the West,
the North from the South.

O mountain, be thou removed forever,
like a scarlet letter scraped
from the forehead of White America!

Climbing the Mountain Boldly: King's Theological Method as Paradigm

The compelling theme of the civil rights movement, "We Shall Overcome," is more critical now on the eve of the twenty-first century than it was more than forty years ago.[21] The song itself is a profile in courage, not only worth remembering, but even more worth internalizing in the heart and soul of America. Theologians and historians of the civil rights movement remind us that the prophetic voice of Martin Luther King, Jr., was the decisive moral force that captured the imagination and energy of countless peoples of every tongue, clan, village, and nation in our global community: Europeans, Russians, Africans, Native Americans, Latinos, Asians, Pacific Islanders, and all the "ethnic shades" of God's rainbow humanity.

At the global level, this humble Baptist preacher—intellectually nurtured in a middle-class home of Southern black aristocracy and religious piety—was the chief leader of a movement that, inevitably, became the norm and alternative paradigm of social change for marginalized and oppressed peoples around the world. Now at the center of King's theological method, as I see it, is the bold vision of the "beloved community." In the struggle to climb the mountain of racism, what is the essential message of this bold vision? In the human struggle to achieve self-fulfillment and wholeness, we may simply ask, methodologically, what is the character of the beloved community? Can it ease the perennial pain experienced by blacks and other

---

[21]Cf. Vincent Harding's *Hope and History: Why We Must Share the Story of the Movement* (Maryknoll: Orbis Books, 1990), pp. 3–5; 28–82.

people of color, at the hands of white racism in America? Well, to raise hard questions means that we must, indeed, attempt to fashion some response. Despite the mountainous situation of racism in America, King's faith and theological stance reflected hope over despair, in that he had a vision for society rooted in the biblical notion of the kingdom of God, especially as disclosed in the New Testament teachings of Jesus. Through many of his speeches, sermons, and lectures, King explained it this way:

> Jesus took over the phrase "the Kingdom of God," but he changed its meaning. He refused entirely to be the kind of a Messiah that his contemporaries expected. Jesus made love the mark of sovereignty. Here we are left with no doubt as to Jesus' meaning. The Kingdom of God will be a society in which men and women live as children of God should live. It will be a kingdom controlled by the law of love...Many have attempted to say that the ideal of a better world will be worked out in the next world. But Jesus taught men to say, "Thy will be done in earth, as it is in heaven." Although the world seems to be in a bad shape today, we must never lose faith in the power of God to achieve his purpose.[22]

At other junctures of his intellectual pilgrimage, he argued that one can struggle against the forces of racial bigotry, poverty, and ignorance because in the "beloved community" there is no place for ethnic strife or hatred. "Christianity repudiates racism," said King. Then he went on to critique the clerical and professional custodians of middle-class Christianity in contemporary society—especially the racial hypocrisy and moralism that disguise themselves at Sunday

---

[22]Kenneth L. Smith and Ira G. Zepp, Jr., *Search for the Beloved Community: The Thinking of Martin Luther King, Jr.* (Valley Forge, Pennsylvania: Judson Press, 1974), p. 129. It is important to mention that in scholarly circles, as well as in the wider global community, the interest in King's critical thought has grown by leaps and bounds over the last two decades. This profound theological interest is reflected in recent scholarly works such as J. H. Cone's *Martin and Malcolm and America: A Dream or a Nightmare?* (Maryknoll: Orbis Books, 1991); John J. Ansbro's *Martin Luther King, Jr.: The Making of a Mind* (Maryknoll: Orbis Books, 1982); David J. Garrow's *Bearing the Cross: Martin Luther King, Jr., and the Southern Christian Leadership Conference* (New York: Vintage Books, 1988); and Noel Leo Erskine's *King among the Theologians* (Cleveland: Pilgrim Press, 1994).

morning worship, with little relevance to the social struggle and pain many oppressed peoples feel on Monday morning. He wrote:

> For so many Christians, Christianity is a Sunday activity having no relevancy for Monday and the church is little more than a secular social club having a thin veneer of religiosity. Jesus is an ancient symbol whom we do the honor of calling Christ, and yet his Lordship is neither affirmed nor acknowledged by our substantive lives.[23]

Thus King's conception of the "beloved community" was a prophetic vision that linked biblical teachings about the "Kingdom of God" with the social evils of racism, poverty, and classism in both church and society.

Concretely speaking, I suspect that the attractiveness of King's theological method, in dealing with the mountain of racism, revolves around the analytical and interpretive categories of what I call *particularism and universalism*. In the first place, by employing the interpretive category of particularism I mean to suggest that his theology is contextual, that it takes seriously the social condition of black oppression and suffering in America. I think that King knew all too well the cruel reality of what it means to be "black" in white America, and the conflicting valuations and social stigma associated with skin color. The slippery mountain of racism tends to perpetuate a view that "if you are white, you're all right; if you are brown, stick around; but if you are black, stay back!" Traditionally and currently, blacks are still, in the words of King, "the first fired and the last hired." Yet the irony of the matter is that while blacks in America are still being *held down*, they cannot be *held back*. There is a moral force loose in the world, deeply rooted in the redemptive promises of God, that can no longer be resisted or ultimately crushed.[24]

In the second place, the genius of the theology of King is its *decisive particularity*. Theological particularism in the black religious experience means that one refuses to sidestep the brutality of racism and its effect upon our national moral character. Given the dialectics of black life in

---

[23]Lotte Hoskins, ed., *"I Have a Dream: The Quotations of Martin Luther King, Jr.* (New York: Grosset and Dunlap, 1968), p. 117.

[24]Enoch H. Oglesby, *God's Divine Arithmetic: Christian Ethics for Preaching and Evangelism* (Nashville: Townsend Press, 1985), p. 69.

white America, King often spoke of the importance of having a "tough mind and tender heart." Theoretically considered, I suspect that what we see, in regard to the issue of racism, is the tough-mindedness of a pastor-theologian. For King, racism is a cancerous evil in the body-politic of our society. Indeed, it is an evil which endures in mainstream denominational white churches. Despite apparent advances and even significant external changes in the last two decades, the mountain of racism remains. In large measure it is only the external appearances which have changed. As one brother put it, "Racism is still alive and well, man; it has only moved from the housetop to the basement." Of course, the basement—that is to say, at the foundation—is where it can do the most damage![25]

Thus, the *particularity* of King's theological method enables us to more fully discern the signs of the time. It enables us to see that racial prejudice is part of the cultural and socioeconomic matrix in America. His theology seems to suggest that this evil reality today is an integral part of the American bourgeois trinity: Capitalism, Racism, and Sexism. Of course, there were many other "isms" that King attempted to address in his ethical and theological reflections upon the American social system. For example, I suspect that "militarism" would rank very high, as well as the moral dilemmas inherent in Marxism *vis-à-vis* capitalism. In a comparative manner, King observed:

> Truth is not to be found either in traditional capitalism or in Marxism. Each represents a partial truth. Historically, capitalism failed to discern the truth in collective enterprise and Marxism failed to see the truth in individual enterprise. Nineteenth-century capitalism failed to appreciate that life is social, and Marxism failed, and still fails, to see that life is individual and social. The Kingdom of God is neither the thesis of individual enterprise nor the antithesis of collective enterprise, but a synthesis which reconciles the truth of both.[26]

In the third place, particularism in the ethico-theological thought of King seems to bring into sharp focus, as we have seen, the cruciality

---

[25]Ibid., p. 69.
[26]Martin Luther King, Jr., *Strength to Love* (New York: Harper & Row, 1963), pp. 114–123.

of the kingdom of God motif. Here, we see that the motif of the kingdom of God, (*basileia*, i.e., the reign of God in and over all creation), is an informing biblical paradigm for King with respect to ideologies of both capitalism and Marxism. Accordingly, it is the breaking in of the kingdom that enables Christians and ethically sensitive persons to radically critique the political and economic systems of the modern world. For King, the kingdom motif means that God declares judgment not only on the cult of racism in white middle class mainline churches, but also on structures of economic exploitation as well. "The profit motive, when it is the sole basis of an economic system," says King, "encourages a cutthroat competition and selfish ambition that inspires men to be more concerned about making a living than making a life."[27]

In essence, the result of King's theological particularism is, as I see it, the critical judgment brought to bear upon all unjust social and economic structures that deny God's kingdom and plan for justice and freedom, for human wholeness and the fullness of life. Hence, the kingdom motif in King's thought seems to critique our actions, both internally and externally, in the light of racist and exploitative structures.

To summarize the idea of *particularism* as an interpretive method in the theology of King, two comments seem appropriate. First, King's theological perspective speaks of the need to eradicate the cancer of white racism from our churches, social institutions, and national life. Second, theological particularism in the thinking of King means that God sides with the poor and dispossessed in spite of, and because of, the marginality of blacks and other minorities in American society.

King's theology also sets forth the theme of universalism. I think King held the moral conviction that God's word affirms and proclaims the oneness of the human family—from the first words of Genesis to the "Come, Lord Jesus" of the book of Revelation. The people that make up our "global village"—the haves and have-nots, the disenfranchised, the outcasts, the poor, and the rich, and the young and old of the world community—all represent an object of ultimate concern in the thought of King. He believed that "injustice

---

[27]Ibid., p. 121.

anywhere is a threat to justice everywhere," and that devoted Christians and people of goodwill all over the world must speak out against all forms of oppression. Indeed, the gospel of Jesus Christ requires that we do nothing less—as we move toward maturity and the universal oneness of God's creation in Jesus Christ. King affirms:

> Christians are...bound to recognize the ideal of a world unity in which all barriers of caste and color are abolished. Christianity repudiates racism. The broad universalism standing at the center of the gospel makes both theory and practice of racial injustice morally unjustifiable. Racial prejudice is a blatant denial of the unity which we have in Christ, for in Christ there is neither Jew nor Gentile, bond nor free, Negro nor white.[28]

In short, universalism is an ever-present strand in the thought of King. As a prophetic voice in the cause of freedom, social justice, and personhood, King declared: "Now the judgment of God is upon us, and we must either learn to live together as brothers or we are all going to perish together as fools."

From Credo to Courage

In a multiracial and multicultural society where racism is still a powerful demonic force of exploitation of the poor by the rich in our socioeconomic system, Christians of goodwill can clearly see that the virtue of courage is a scarce commodity. Notwithstanding, the virtue of courage is what we must have in order to be equipped in climbing the treacherous mountain of racism in the United States. In short, the ethical imperative for diverse communities of faith is to move from *credo* to *courage*. In the former, the Latin word for creed, *credo*, anchors the etymological character of "credo" which literally means "I believe" or a statement of religious belief such as the Nicene Creed—often sung, for instance, as a part of the liturgy in certain ecclesiological traditions. As a mere statement of principle, the Latin verb, *credere*, or "to believe," is qualitatively different from the ethical norm of *praxis*, which means "an act"

For example, we may illustrate this perennial ethical tension in ethnic relations between "believing" and "doing" by looking at this

---

[28]Ibid., p. 119.

confessional scenario. One statement may read: "*believe* that all people are of equal worth in the eyes of God." A second statement may read: "I *treat* all people equal, because all of us are of equal worth in the eyes of God." Now which of these provisional and confessional statements would you want your employer to be duty-bound? Here I think that it is reasonable to assume that the thoughtful person or moral agent would, undoubtedly, find a greater affinity and kinship with the second statement. Hence, we are challenged in dealing with the "racism dilemma" in church and society to move from religious confession to moral action, from credo to courage. "Courage may be the most important of all virtues because without it one cannot practice any other virtue with consistency," says Maya Angelou.

Now in the face of racism of the wider society, we may critically ask, "What are the functional lessons of courage, implicit or explicit, in the black church experience today?" I hold the theological viewpoint that these "functional lessons" may take the form of what I call the "*Seven Functional Principles*," which reveal, in part, the heart and soul of black church life in the contemporary American society. While my observations are not intended to be exhaustive, they do, in fact, reflect a certain religio-cultural texture in the fabric of the moral world of African American Christians. In the rhythmic flow from credo to courage, these functional caveats include:

1. *Don't deny the reality of racism.* Denial leads only to more self-deception in the USA and in global society. Every solitary struggle to overcome the "principalities" of racism is a small footprint toward God's justice (Rom. 8:38).
2. *I wouldn't have a religion that I couldn't "feel" sometimes*: In the African American church experience, people of color do not separate "feeling" from "intellect"—as if to embrace some Aristotelian dualism of an unholy dichotomy between mind and body. On the contrary, Christians of the black church experience are more likely to affirm a religion of Jesus that *links* "feeling" and "faith," "intellect" and "action" in the struggle to climb the mountain of racism and to achieve authentic freedom and racial equality.

This moral lesson or principle also arises from our religious music, for example, in the song "Every Time I Feel the Spirit Moving in My Heart I Will Pray" (cf. Luke 4:18–19).

3. *Don't be quick to judge* the overt actions or attitudes of another, in a racially conflicted situation, without first probing motive (Mt. 7:1–2). Rather, engage the other person in the *praxis* of love to avoid confusion and conflict in ethnic relations.

4. *Respect cultural and theological differences* as a gift to be *celebrated*, not as a problem to be avoided. The new society is all about *being*, living as if the new order has appeared upon the present order. Thus affirm the new being, *esse quam videri*, "to be rather than to seem" (Rom. 12:1–2; Rev. 21:1–5ff).

5. *The invitation to do battle in the moral struggle against racism cannot be won by black soldiers alone:* but rather it must be engaged in by all peoples who love justice and are disturbed by the tug of conscience. I've never seen a racist that God didn't love; thus no human being is beyond Christ's redemption (Rom 10:9; 1 Pet. 2:29).

6. *The "cutting edge" of reality has two fighting sisters:* Rage and Hope. "Sister Rage" of the black church family is painfully disturbed about the way things *are*, in our predominantly white racist society; but "Sister Hope" is determined, by God's grace, to change the things that *are*, that ought not to be. Historically, the black church has been that sort of "cutting edge" reality whose self-understanding or mission is not simply the mere saving of black souls, but the liberation and humanization of the whole world. Between the sisters of "rage and hope" stands the fragile humanity of us all—symbolized in a child. Hence, the African proverb reminds us: "It takes a whole village to raise a child!" (Isa. 11:6; Mt. 18:2)

7. *The dialectical movement from credo to courage requires character to "name" the mountain:* Thus the act of "naming" racism is, undoubtedly, the first honest step at the base of the mountain. It is imperative, or so it seems to me, that Christians the world over have the courage to "name" racism for what it is: a sin against God and humanity. This caveat recognizes the sobering truth that the process of dismantling the mountain of racism—stone by stone—involves a

collective effort which demands attitudinal and structural changes from the bottom up—beginning within the home, church, public schools, universities and seminaries, and other critical institutions that touch the lives of us all. In short, the courage to "name" the mountain in these various "locations" within our sociocultural system requires a certain amount of character amid certain menacing tribulations (Rom. 5:1–5).

Because the Old Ones in the black church often kept alive the diversity and richness of our religio-cultural heritage by storytelling, I want to collect my meandering thoughts by sharing a folk tale.

In reflecting upon racism as a mountain and the role of the church in light of the total legacy of Martin Luther King, Jr., I am reminded of what I wish to call the modern parable of "Tom the Grasshopper." Once upon a time, there was one who bore the name Umoia, which means "unity," or "togetherness." Umoia was a very strong individual of pride, dignity, and intelligence. Umoia lived in the deep green forest of plenty, in harmony with nature and the serenity of village life. Umoia was a happy human being. But then a strangeness began to blow through the winds of history. As the drama of this modern parable unfolds, that which was serene and fun all at once turned into frantic anxiety and fear. Happiness turned into heartache, and noble triumph gave way to cultural tragedy, as Umoia, the noble one of unity, was stripped of his name and given a surname: "Tom the Grasshopper."

Now, before Tom the Grasshopper became "Tom," he would spend many joyous hours in the deep green forest without a care in the world. As the modern parable unravels, we observe that Tom, the Grasshopper—without warning or intent—fell into a large jar, with an automatic lid on top. There he stayed for more than 250 years until his friend, Hodges, came along and took the lid off the top of the jar. Having become conditioned by the lid, Tom was unaware that the lid was actually off and subsequently stayed within the jar for another 100 years. You see, Tom the Grasshopper had become socially adjusted to the environment inside—a painful price for survival!

Finally, there came along in due time another friend, which we shall call the "moral force," and he said:

Hey, Tom! Hey, Tom! Way down there, don't you know the lid
is off the jar…? Hop on out, man, into the land of the freedom! You need not be bound by the false lid. You really are
free! Praise God! Hallelujah! Hallelujah! The chains have been
broken from your legs and mind forever. Hop on out!

In this modern parable, the life and theological method of Martin Luther King, Jr., symbolize the "moral force," the third option,
the alternative vision for the poor and the oppressed and all people
of goodwill who love justice and peace in the world. After so much
agony and pain, of waiting and praying, of hoping and dying, the
church of Jesus Christ has a window of opportunity to tell the hurting ones—whether they be red, yellow, black or white—that the
treacherous mountain of racism is not the *final act*; the vision beyond the mountain summons us all to higher ground. For the hurting victims of systemic racism, the eschatological vision implicit in
King's idea of the beloved community shouts from the *mountain-top*
to us in the valley, "Brothers and Sisters, from every land and tongue:
Let go! Be not afraid! God has allowed us to scale the mountain—
I've seen the promised land…and we as a people will get to the
promised land." Ethically considered, I do not think that the vision
itself takes on flesh and blood until ordinary people—from every
ethnic background—have the courage to practice justice and kindness in human community.

2

Racism and the Search for an Ethical Method

*If there is no struggle, there is no progress .... This struggle may be
a moral one; or it may be a physical one; or it may be both moral
and physical; but it must be a struggle.*

—Frederick Douglass

*There remains an experience of incomparable value. We have for
once learnt to see the great events of world history from below, from
the perspective of the outcast, the suspects, the maltreated, the
powerless, the oppressed, the reviled—in short, from the perspective
of those who suffer.*

—Dietrich Bonhoeffer

Relating Christian Ethics and Ethnicity

The African American spirit of moral resistance to residual forms
of racism in the United States is a critical yearning on the part of
oppressed people to free themselves from the domination and control of their captors. While the racism dilemma has been an enduring moral problem for us in the whole of Western culture, it is

33

important to note that Euro-American theologians, philosophers, and religious ethicists have been reluctant—in large measure—to tackle this issue head-on. Because black people and other people of color have been viewed by whites, in some degree, to be "less intelligent," "less hardworking" and "less productive," the tendency has been to simply ignore and distort their substantive contributions— whether in art, literature, religion or science—to world civilization.

For example, I would suspect that this tendency in the Anglo-American perspective in regard to doing theology and ethics may be partially rooted, historically, in the doctrine of white supremacy, which generally interpreted the subordinate position of blacks in the dominant sociocultural system as due to immutable psychobiological differences between the races.[1] In a provocative new book, *The Spirituality of African Peoples: The Search for a Common Moral Discourse*, Peter Paris illustrates this moral failure of perspective on racism by citing the critique from the African scholar J. Ki-Zerbo:

> Racism is a scourge that is capable of taking on a multiplicity of forms, from the most discreetly concealed to the most bloodthirsty, as in the case of the slave trade and the Second World War. Like a living fossil, it bides its time, buried in the subconscious of hundreds of millions of people, until it re-awakens in the shape of pseudo-scientific doctrines and claims; for example, that everything remarkable about Africa must be of foreign origin, because Africans themselves have never invented anything. This attitude was carried to such lengths that the main issue raised in connection with the masterpieces of life sculpture was that of finding out what foreign peoples had managed to travel as far as that region in order to produce such works of art.[2]

---

[1]George D. Kelsey, *Racism and the Christian Understanding of Man* (New York: Charles Scribner's Sons, 1965), pp. 82–86.

[2]Cited in Peter J. Paris, *The Spirituality of African Peoples: The Search for a Common Moral Discourse.* (Minneapolis: Fortress Press, 1995), pp. 8–9. This critique of a Eurocentric philosophy of colonialism, dehumanization, and domination is very similar to that of Cheikh Anta Diop in his efforts to show how the positive intellectual contributions and cultural artifacts of African peoples were stripped away or excluded by the majority of European scholars and historians of the modern era. For further study see his classic work, *The African Origin of Civilization: Myth or Reality* (Westport, Connecticut: Lawrence Hill, 1974), pp. 1–53.

The new wave of African American scholarship in particular, along with the enterprise of theological education in "Third World" countries, has significantly called into question the way we do Christian social ethics in the post-colonial era of the modern world. A growing cadre of African scholars, theologians, artists, and black intellectuals are forming a *critical united front* to resist the hegemonic imposition of the ideology of white racism.[3] In terms of social sources for moral resistance, one can say, candidly, that these are "the best of times and the worst of times" for Christian communities of faith the world over. Thus the climate of the times demands that we raise and revisit again a whole battery of critical questions in the theater of American culture—particularly in regard to what it means to be faithful in grappling with the slippery mountain of racism. For example, what is the relation between Christian ethics and ethnicity? What is the nature and task of ethics given the situation of racism in America? Are there certain provisional insights or functional approaches to ethics that may assist the church in dismantling racism? Is one ethical approach to individual and social decision making just as good as another? For people of goodwill and Christian conscience, what consequences must be faced if we fail to climb this "treacherous mountain"? After all, what, in a defining moment, is Christian ethics? For us to raise these critical ethico-theological questions does not mean, necessarily, that we can provide the correct and perfect answers; but rather, the burden of ethical discourse requires that we be honest in our response, unrelenting in our spirit to "know the truth," and faithful in our convictions to *act* upon that which we know as moral agents of a freeing and unfailing God.

In any event, let us come now to the table of some foundational understandings of the nature of ethics. In the first place, I hold a basic view that theory and practice are always united in ethical discourse, if the real concerns and struggles of the poor and marginalized ones can, in fact, be addressed. In the second place, the force of this view, rooted as it were in the biblical understanding of God's righteousness, demands that our faith—often expressed in flowery "words"—be put into moral action. For Christians, just as there is no right way to interpret the *wrong* of racism, there is no moral

---

[3]Ibid., p. 209.

legitimation for separating "word" from "deed" in the unfolding drama of biblical faith. Scripture teaches us this important moral lesson: "Little children, let us not love in word or speech but in deed and in truth" (1 John 3:18). In the third place, it seems to me that the real point of the moral lesson is self-evident when it comes to the problem of ethnic relations in the dominant host culture, namely, the mere "speech" of ethnic inclusivity is qualitatively different from that of the "deed." The Bible admonished us to work intentionally at the latter, without ignoring the former. To be sure, we must ponder and struggle more seriously with the question of how best to envision the ethical task in regard to the dilemmas of racism in the United States.

Understanding Ethics and the Mountain of Racism

While the divergence of perspectives is widespread on the question of ethical task, notice must be given to the prior functional question, "What is ethics?"

Conceptually, we must argue ethics is not a pure matter of logic and theory, but of life and struggle, as the moral agent seeks to understand why so many people, seemingly, catch the "mountain fever" of racism in the United States! *Ethics* is disciplined reflection upon the moral basis of individual and social decision making, action, and conduct in human community. In a manner of speaking, ethics is the critical study of values, customs, and modes of personal and institutional patterns of behavior in modern society, in the light of what *ought to be*. Theoretically considered, the ethicist engages in normative thinking about the nature and foundational character of conduct in the attempt to better understand why people "behave" and "respond" as they do—under varying types of circumstances in history, especially in regard to the phenomenon of racism in our time.

In the sort of world in which we live, Christians of North America are concerned about issues and moral problems that affect us all. Broadly speaking, at nearly every juncture of human life we are engaged in some form of decision making about religion, politics, economics, education, church and family life. We are creatures that practice the art of moral choice, whether we do this with intentionality or in a sporadic way; from the crack of dawn to the whispers of the night, the human being is doing ethics. In regard to racism, what is at stake is understanding the ethical task for those who take seriously the essential claims of black theology in North America. One of the claims of black theology is that white theologians and moral thinkers have largely ignored the corpus of black experience as a legitimate point of theological discourse and decision making, in light of that which is good, right, and just in human society.[4] At the fundamental level we must raise again the question of not only "What is ethics?" but "What has ethics to do with the situation of oppression in North America? For Christians and secular persons, what has ethics to do with theology and the human struggle for liberation?"

First of all, the word *ethics* is derived from the Greek *ethos*, and related to the Latin term *mos* (from which we derive *moral*.) The former refers to a stall or dwelling. The latter means custom or usage as prescribed by the moral practices of a given community. Thus the term ethos refers to a web of values or beliefs that functions as cement in holding together our sense of community, moral identity, and culture. Thus we may say that our decisions about right and wrong, good and evil, appropriate and inappropriate behavior are fundamentally ethos questions. Secondly, good conduct or a sense of justice and freedom are assumed by some ethical theologians as the basis upon which human society rests. The ethical problem here, however, is discernment of the ethos, and those conflicting forces that either pervert or morally corrupt the ethos and make it less than fully human. What I am trying to suggest, as we struggle with the issues raised by black theology, is that the slippery mountain of racism, oppression, and injustice have distorted our fundamental sense of community (ethos) among North American churches.[5]

Furthermore, I think that one of the key contributions of black theology in the discussion of racism, relative to the ethical task, is the issue of the historical context. The awesome reality for black and other people of color in the United States is one of oppression and socioeconomic exploitation. Thus, any viable conceptualization

---

[4]Enoch H. Oglesby, "Toward a Black Ethical Theology" in Deane Wilborn Ferm, ed., *Liberation Theology: North American Style* (New York: International Religious Foundation, 1987), pp. 207–208.
[5]Ibid., p. 209.

of the ethical task for Christians must reflect sensibility to the pain and suffering of people as generated by the sociohistorical context. Put another way, racism in America is not *ahistorical*; it is not a transcendent reality beyond the boundaries of the social structure. To the contrary, the ethical task of discernment, as informed by biblical faith, places the phenomenon of racism *within* history. Racism persists *within* the dominant social, economic, and political structures of American life. Thus the ethical task of discernment is critically related to black theology, because it suggests that racism as an idolatrous mountain also exists *within* ourselves: in the campgrounds of our attitudes, values, customs, and practices. To borrow the language of eminent sociologist Robert Bellah, racism is not a matter of the head but of the heart. I think, therefore, that racism in the United States has to do, fundamentally, with the "habits of the heart." Now in the Christian community of faith, this makes the ethical task of discernment even more crucial.

In the perennial search for a viable ethical approach to the problem of racism, I find the volume *Bible and Ethics in the Christian Life* by Bruce C. Birch and Larry L. Rasmussen useful for the reader. This is especially true for examining the categories that shed further light on the ethical task. They identify the following *tasks* of Christian ethics:

> .... a descriptive task, a critical task, and a normative task. The first seeks simply to comprehend and describe the moral life as it is actually lived. The second makes critical inquiry about it. The third attempts to state the proper content and procedures for living it as it ought to be lived.

> The descriptive task covers a number of different concerns. How in fact do people make ethical choices and what are the qualities of character which they embody? What are the operative creeds and the moralities by which they live?

> The third task, belonging to what is often called "normative" or "constructive" ethics, is that of providing recommended content and method for the moral life and supplying sound

supporting reasons for these. Normative ethics attempts to say what the good life is, what characterizes the good person and the good society, what marks the right decision and action on a particular matter.[6]

Here the overarching concern of the authors is for moral agents to struggle with who we are and ought to be as persons or groups with unique histories in the American sociocultural system. In short, the ethical task always demands that we assess critically—in light of the situation of racism in the United States—the "concrete choices and deeds in particular circumstances on specific moral issues and problems."[7]

Black Theology and the Ethical Task

Because of the situation of racism and oppression we have discovered in recent years that those who do black theology must also do ethics, not in some universal context, but within an African American Christian context, for the good of the whole church.

Logically we ask: "What, then is the ethical task?" Formally, I think that the ethical task is twofold, especially for those concerned about the theology of liberation for the poor and the oppressed in American society. Hence, the first formal task is clarification of the funky facts of life with respect to the black religious experience in America. The second formal task is interpretation of the meaning of Christian faith for the people whose history is clouded by the dialectics of chattel slavery and racial segregation. I agree with Joseph Washington's observation that "the only 'status' Blacks have had in America was in slavery. It is against the American faith for Blacks to gain status in America apart from the shackles of slavery."[8] What I am suggesting here is that the formal task of ethics has always been to illuminate and reflect upon the human condition by clarifying the moral values and beliefs that make for life over against death. For the black Christian community in North America, the reality of

---

[6]Bruce C. Birch and Larry L. Rasmussen, *Bible and Ethics in the Christian Life* (Minneapolis: Augsburg Publishing House, 1976) pp. 82–83.

[7]Ibid., p. 82.

[8]See Deane William Ferm, ed., *Liberation Theology: North American Style* (New York: International Religious Foundation, Inc., 1987), p. 209.

slavery made for death. By stark contrast, the reality of the gospel made for life and freedom. To be sure, there is a close connection between the task of ethics and black theology found among those who seek to be faithful to the gospel. The interpretive task of ethics means that black people in North America seem to experience the gospel of Jesus Christ as a gospel of redemption and empowerment. Therefore, we may define the task of a black Christian ethics as the discernment of radical freedom for the moral life, initiated by the redeeming love of God in Jesus Christ, for the sake of all humanity, especially the marginalized.

Beyond clarification and interpretation, I suspect that critical theological discourse would suggest that the ultimate task of ethics—given the situations of oppression in North America—is the disposition that all moral values must be evaluated in terms of their capacity to liberate human beings. It would seem that for many black theologians and church leaders the gospel of Jesus Christ most significantly affirms this disposition. As St. Paul eloquently said in his letter to the Galatians, "For freedom Christ has set us free. Stand firm therefore, and do not submit again to a yoke of slavery" (Gal. 5:1).

When the rhetoric of ethical reflection clears in the public arena of black theology and church life, what we find is a powerful ethic of liberation derived from the gospel of Jesus Christ and from a peculiar God of the Bible who sides with the poor and the oppressed.[9]

Thus we cannot minimize the importance of understanding the ethical task. Ethics and theology are inseparable for churches concerned about the demands of liberation in North America. Indeed, ethics in this sense is derived from theology and the church's reflection on the meaning and practice of divine liberation in the world. As Cone reminds us, Christian theology asks, "Who is God?" and ethics asks, "What must we do?" For many morally sensitive persons in church and society, theology means that we must deal with the God question essentially from the perspective of human suffering and oppression. Theology is talking to God about our wounds and our hurts. Theology is God-talk. Comparatively, ethics

---

[9]Ibid., p. 210.

is disciplined reflection upon God-talk for human conduct. Hence, ethics, in the sense of divine praxis, is God-walk.

Discerning the ethical task means knowing the pivotal links between each informing discipline in the life of faith of the church. In understanding the ethical task for North American churches, three brief caveats seem appropriate. First, understanding the ethical task in the community of faith means "speaking the truth" about the realities of oppression and the need for divine liberation. With few exceptions, black theologians point out that white scholars and moral thinkers in America have failed to ground their interpretation of Christian ethics in an analysis of God's liberating activity. It seems to me, therefore, that the burden of the ethical task is to "speak the truth" about the doing of ethics on the contemporary American scene and its tendency to separate the politics of God from the politics of oppression. Hence, the burden of the ethical task involves nothing less than speaking the truth to power. "For our struggle is not against enemies of blood and flesh but against the rulers, against the authorities…" says Paul (Eph. 6:12). Secondly, understanding the ethical task involves "speaking the truth with love." The norm of love is the highest virtue of Christian ethics. But for the Christian community, it is a virtue whose faithfulness is legitimated by the doing of justice, feeding the hungry, clothing the naked, and a distributing wealth and power humanely. Normatively, the task of "speaking the truth with love" aims at the establishment of justice and righteousness on the part of the poor and oppressed in the land.[10] Jesus reminded his disciples that love must be the motivation of moral action. He asserted, "Love the Lord your God with all your heart, with all your soul, with all your mind." Put another way, the individual person who is faithful to the ethical task discerns the close connection between love and the struggle for justice and freedom. Thirdly, understanding the ethical task for churches of North America involves contextual analysis of the reality of racism. Black theologians and laypeople as well point out that racism is endemic to white America. Racism per se denies the presence of God and produces misery, hate, and alienation in the body of Christ. Because racism is a sin against God and humanity, the burden of the ethical

---

[10]Ibid., p. 211.

task becomes even more important. It is a task of digging and honest appraisal of the phenomenon of white racism in our midst. Let us now turn to a few noted theologians and philosophers who may shed further light on the problem of methodology in ethnic relations.

Martin Buber

In our continuous search for a viable ethical method to address the atrocities of racial bigotry, ethnic strife, cruelty, violence—and on the global scale—after the death camps, Auschwitz, and the injustice of the internment of Japanese Americans, and after the necessary death of our "childhood's faith," we come to the emerging personality and prophetic thought of Martin Buber. Like Rauschenbusch of the social gospel movement, the critical ethico-theological thought of Martin Buber, for example, exerted a positive shadow over the struggle for black liberation, particularly in light of the formation of the ethics and theology of Martin Luther King, Jr.

With a peculiar shade of irony, Buber poses the critical life and death question of ethical discourse:

> Dare we recommend to the survivors of Oswiecim, the Job of the gas chambers: "Call to Him, for He is kind, for His mercy endures forever"?[11]

Reflecting on the evils of ethnic injustice, racism, and involuntary suffering implicit in human existence, Lowell Streiker, in his book *The Promise of Buber*, has made the following assertion in regard to the theology and ethical sensibility of Martin Buber:

> .... the only basis for affirming the meaningfulness of life in the face of the insurmountable evils of human existence is the recognition that man's sufferings are also the sufferings of God, that man's struggle to realize good despite all that opposes him is at the same time God's ongoing creation of order out of primal chaos. The redemptive process through which the harmony and reunification are achieved is a divine-human

[11]Lowell D. Streiker, *The Promise of Buber* (Philadelphia: J. B. Lippincott, 1969), p. 66.

undertaking, a partnership which exposes both man and God to opposition, defeat, and pain. Unless God himself participates in the heartaches and sorrows of man's earthly state, then all striving is in vain.[12]

It is only a glimpse into the obvious to suggest that as a Jewish theologian and moral philosopher, Martin Buber was one of the most revolutionary religious thinkers of his age. According to Streiker, Buber the moral philosopher is remembered by many names: "philosopher of dialogue," "Jewish existentialist," "utopian socialist," "religious reformer," "mystic," "theological anthropologist," "man of peace".[13] The list of intellectual commendations may go on and on, *ad infinitum*. However, for our reflections on the viability of the search for a usable ethical method to struggle with the phenomenon of racism, his theory of selfhood as "subject" rather than "object" is promising—in light of the black condition of suffering in white America. For Buber, the God of faith and struggle does not call us to a self-centered hunger for a "mystical religion" that transcends the mundane problems of historical existence, but rather an understanding of God that invites "dialogue" and struggle with the moral problems and ambiguities in our fragmented world. In the critical socioethical thought of Buber, religion is not a "gatekeeper" for the world's pain and suffering, but a transforming reality of the head and heart, leading each person as a moral agent to deep levels of relationality and "dialogue" in the lived world of experience. Religion summons us to partnership in the work of the Divine; religion is not a set of dogmatic propositions about the character of God as transcendent reality, but a relationship to God marked by trust, unconditional love, moral struggle, and an attitude of expectancy in the day-to-day life of the person in human community.

In any event, Buber's theoretical construct of the moral life reflects two basic orientational attitudes toward reality: *I-Thou* and *I-It*. This analytical distinction is undoubtedly familiar to many of us in the broad enterprise of theological education who daily struggle with the dialectical and ultimate questions of meaning and purpose, identity and authority, power and vulnerability, hope and despair, and liberation and

---

[12]Ibid., p. 66.
[13]Ibid., p. 12.

reconciliation on the part of people from diverse religious and cultural backgrounds. Here it seems to me that what is paramount, however, is understanding these two basic attitudes toward reality, in light of the phenomenon of racism. First, the *"I-It"* attitude portrays the self as alienated reality: fragmented, separated, demoralized, de-centered beings in our world of brokenness and death. The *"I-It"* relation imprisons the self without a jail cell or prison walls—by virtue of reducing all human life and thought to the objective world of "it-ness."

For example, in this predictable, twisted scheme of *I-It* reality, the slave and the slave-master are, strangely, equal—but the latter is virtually unaware because of the deceptive and insidious power of white racism. The essential irony of the *I-It* attitude, for suffering humanity, according to Buber, is simply this: the one who lives with *It* alone becomes a non-being. By contrast, the *I-Thou* attitude designates the presence of persons-in-community; the *I-Thou* attitude affirms the value of relationships *between* persons and not objects. Unlike the *I-It* objectivity, the *I-Thou* places value on mutuality, reciprocity, and the entrustment of "selves" in the context of human community. The "thou" or the "I-you" is a child of God—a moral being called to live in harmony and love with one another in our fragile global village. With some implications for the black condition, Lowell Streiker summarizes the two basic attitudes in this manner:

> The attitude of *I-Thou* designates a relationship between subjects or persons. The English translation is somewhat unfortunate, since the word "Thou" is usually reserved for prayer. In order to overcome the sanctimonious tone of "Thou," we should think of the relation of reciprocity and mutuality of person to person which Buber has in mind as "I-You." Although I live by virtue of my *I-It* objectivity, it is only when I address another being as "you" and am myself so addressed that my distinctive nature, my life as a person standing in relation to another person, is realized.
>
> That which happens between an *I* and a *You* determines the uniqueness of a man, the never to be repeated meaning of his life. It is through the *I-You* relationship that personality emerges.[14]

---

[14]Ibid., p. 35.

Walter Rauschenbusch

Few twentieth-century theologians and moral thinkers have exerted greater influence over our fundamental orientation to social problems in the life and faith of the church in American society than Walter Rauschenbusch. With the publication of his first book, *Christianity and the Social Crisis* (1907), Walter Rauschenbusch gave credence to and established a theological basis for engaging the major social questions of his time. These critical social questions tended to include: (a) the problem of economic injustice in the work force, especially in regard to patterns of rapid growth in industry and commerce at the turn of the twentieth century; (b) the increased alienation and exploitation experienced by people of the laboring class and the apparent inadequacy on the part of the church to respond to such a pattern of collective suffering; and (c) the concern for the idea of the kingdom of God as an ethical imperative for motivating the church to become involved in the "social crisis."

Rauschenbusch was insistent upon the importance of passion and emotion in making the gospel of Jesus Christ relevant to economic and social conditions affecting a the laboring class. For Rauschenbusch's ethic and ecclesiology, the idea of the kingdom of God was the central object of Christian preaching and evangelism, and the motivating force for seeking justice and the amelioration of the economic condition in the wider society. In terms of cultural expression the idea of the kingdom was similar to a sort of covenantal brotherhood of baptized believers. From the preamble of one initial document we find these covenantal words:

> The Spirit of God is moving men in our generation toward a better understanding of the idea of the Kingdom of God on earth. Obeying the thought of our Master, and trusting in the power and guidance of the Spirit, we form ourselves into a Brotherhood of the Kingdom, in order to re-establish this idea in the thought of the church, and to assist in its practical realization in the life of the world.[15]

---

[15]Winthrop S. Hudson, ed., *Walter Rauschenbusch: Selected Writings* (New York: Paulist Press, 1984), p. 25.

The idea of the "Kingdom of God" in the ethical thought of Rauschenbusch reflected many changes in the history of Christianity. One sense in which the term has been used is simply to designate the quality of the "inner life of the Spirit which...constitutes the highest gift of Christianity."[16] In another sense, Rauschenbusch associated the notion of the kingdom with the mission of the church to be a channel through which the ethical impulse of God's righteousness can be poured out upon the lot of suffering humanity. He wrote:

> We must recognize the importance of a living church within the Kingdom. It must not dwindle. It is the channel through which ethical impulses pour into humanity from God. Yet the church and the Kingdom are not identical. We are the church as we worship together; we are the Kingdom as we live justly and lovingly with one another....
>
> But finally, *we must insist that the Kingdom is not only in heaven but is to come to earth*; that *while it begins in the depths of the heart, it is not to stay there; that the church does not embrace all* the forces of the *Kingdom and is but a means for the advancement of the Kingdom*.... The *Kingdom means individual men and women who freely do the will of God*, and who therefore live rightly with their fellowmen. And without a goodly number of such men and women, no plan for a higher social order will have stability enough to work.[17]

While the vision of the kingdom is noble in Rauschenbusch's construction of a Christian social ethic for the church, the vision itself did not, necessarily, include people of African descent. One is made painfully aware of this important point in a critical essay by Preston N. Williams entitled "The Social Gospel and Race Relations: A Case Study of a Social Movement."[18] In this informative

---

[16]Ibid., p. 77.
[17]Ibid., pp. 78–79.
[18]See Preston N. Williams, "The Social Gospel and Race Relations: A Case Study of a Social Movement," in Paul Deats, Jr., ed., *Toward a Discipline of Social Ethics: Essays in Honor of Walter George Muelder* (Boston: Boston University Press, 1972), p. 232.

essay Williams argues the fundamental thesis that "the Social gospel not only spoke weakly to the question of race but that it helped to create a method of analysis that makes more difficult, even today, a solution to the racial problem."[19]

In the light of our perennial search for a viable ethical method to combat racism, we must observe here that the majority of liberal Anglo-Saxon Protestant theologians did not address the social problem of "race" or ethnicity as a central category for ethical analysis in American society. I think that this is one of the most profound ironies in the history of American social Christianity. It seems to me, for example, that both Washington Gladden and Walter Rauschenbusch—though historically located in different sociopolitical places of ministry and prophetic witness—fell into the same trap of "benign neglect" when it came to the race question. Accordingly, Williams emphatically asserts:

> Washington Gladden, founder of the Social Gospel Movement, the first conscious attempt by the American churches to define the nature of their responsibility for justice in social institutions, was at this time in his prime, having been called in 1882 to the First Congregational Church in Columbus, Ohio. Walter Rauschenbusch, the most influential of the early Social Gospel prophets, was about to begin his career at the edge of Hell's Kitchen. It is interesting that neither of these Northern leaders of social and applied Christianity ever sought to attack vigorously the racism which was present and growing in their society. Why did they not conclude that "Christianizing the Social Order" required a Christianizing of white persons' views regarding the Negro?[20]

In a similar manner, Preston N. Williams argues further, and I think rightly so, that Gladden and Rauschenbusch simply did not speak out consistently about the critical socioethical issues of racism and ethnic division of their day. Parenthetically, the failure of "ethical nerve"—on the part of white liberal theologians and social ethicists to speak out against the mountain of racism—has not changed

---

[19]Ibid., p. 233.
[20]Ibid., p. 233.

significantly as we approach the eve of the twenty-first century. As one morally sensitive black preacher lamented: "The more and more things change, the more they remain the same!" In short, the failure to "name" the systemic problem of racism often leads to a bigger problem—beyond which our current failures simply mirror the historic pattern of benign neglect. Williams puts it this way:

> The failure of Gladden and Rauschenbusch is in part due to the fact that racism was so endemic to American life that it was a "ruling idea of all Americans and every age." S. P. Fullinwider has asserted that it was an important element in the thinking of black intellectuals and clergy during this period; and Thomas F. Gossett has made the same assertion in respect to whites. There seems to be little reason for excusing Gladden and Rauschenbusch from this general indictment. Racism during this period was so flagrant, few if any avoided it—certainly not the men of the Social Gospel.[21]

Paul Lehmann

The fundamental relation of persons to community is one of the most fascinating problems of black religious experience and Christian ethics in the modern world. The perennial search and agony for greater understanding and clarity on the proper method to be used in ethical discourse to unmask the phenomenon of racism cannot ignore the interaction of persons in community. From the perspective of the black religious experience, persons are not separate islands of private ethics without context and cultural heritage. On the contrary, it must be argued that persons are complex social wholes, bearing the marks—symbolically and concretely—of the particular cultural traditions, sentiments, religious values, and ideals of a given community. Concerning the profound symbiotic relation of persons to community, the following African proverb hints at this reality: "I am because we are, and since we are, therefore, I am."[22] It seems to me, however, that the methodological question of ethical discourse on the issue of ethnicity can be

---

[21]Ibid., p. 235.
[22]John S. Mbiti, *African Religions and Philosophies* (New York: Anchor Books, 1970), p. 214.

sharply framed in both church and society, namely: How is the individual related to community in light of the situation of racism in America? Paul Lehmann, in his classic work *Ethics in a Christian Context*, sheds an important light, in my opinion, on this most crucial methodological question.

Fundamentally, the classic ethical question, "What ought I to do?" is the wrong methodological starting point for a people who have been enslaved by their oppressors, violently lynched by their captors, stripped of their indigenous culture and language, dislocated from their spiritual homeland, and forced to live in a strange land behind the presumed curtain of "freedom and democracy." Therefore, the ethical impetus or approach starts with the question, "What am I to do?" in the perennial social context of oppression and dominative white racism. Thus Paul Lehmann, in his book *Ethics in a Christian Context*, enables the moral agent to get a methodological handle on the right questions. Accordingly, the Christian church must be the context for raising the hard ethical questions and concerns that bear relevance for shaping a creative response, for instance, to issues such as racism, sexism, classism, and the other "isms" in the Christian moral life. In defining the methodological landscape of ethical discourse, Lehmann writes:

> . . . . Christian ethics is defined as the disciplined reflection upon the question and its answer: What am I, as a believer in Jesus Christ and as a member of his church, to do? The point of departure is neither vague nor neutral. It is not the common moral sense of mankind, the distilled ethical wisdom of the ages. Not that we can ignore this ethical wisdom, but we do not start with it. Instead, the starting point for Christian thinking about ethics is the fact and the nature of the Christian church. To put it somewhat too sharply: Christian ethics is not concerned with the good, but with what I, as a believer in Jesus Christ and as a member of his church, am to do. Christian ethics, in other words, is oriented toward revelation and not toward morality.[23]

---

[23]Paul Lehmann, *Ethics in a Christian Context* (New York: Harper & Row, 1963), p. 45.

In the agonizing search for a viable method of ethical discourse on racism, Lehmann's constructive proposal is highly suggestive because of its emphasis on the cruciality of *context*. So then, in his critical thought, Christian ethics is *koinonia ethics*.[24] The radical implication of this is that the ethicist is one who takes seriously the historical context of racial bigotry and oppression. Thus, theoretically, the contextualism of Lehmann is one that rejects strict reliance on "moral laws" or axiomatic principles as absolutes in favor of the dynamism of a "koinonia ethic" whose claims seek to penetrate the concrete realities of contemporary society by raising the question of what God is doing in the world, in light of the manifold injustices, sufferings, and moral contradictions inherent in human existence. For Lehmann, the stress is placed on the *contextual* character of koinonia ethics, but it does not rely solely on the situation; rather the situation becomes ethically significant only because of what God has done in Jesus Christ, and because of what God is *now doing* in the world.

In short, Christian ethics, for Lehmann, is critical reflection on the question and its answer: "What am I, as a believer in Jesus Christ and as a member of his church, to do?" I think that this question, obviously, has profound implications for the way we grapple with the problem of racism, today, as a people of God. Such an ethical approach is characterized as *indicative* in contrast to *imperative* ethics. Thus the primary ethical reality of which we must be concerned is not the "divine imperative," but the *human indicative*. We shall return to this point later in our discussion of the phenomenon of racism in the United States.

Reinhold Niebuhr

I first came to appreciate Reinhold Niebuhr when I was an eager and energetic graduate student at Boston University. I found myself curiously challenged by the ethical systems and diverse theologies that paraded across the stage of my critical conscience at a time when being male and black in a Ph.D. program was not an ordinary occurrence! Existentially, I was in search of a viable

---

[24]Ibid., pp. 47–49.

framework in my graduate studies that would be sensitive to, and bear affinity with, the pain and suffering of African Americans and other people of color. In the course of my intellectual pilgrimage I had seriously studied the writings of Karl Marx, W.E.B. DuBois, Malcolm X, Martin Luther King, Jr., and James H. Cone. But then I discovered, like a hidden pearl of great price, the Christian ethics of Reinhold Niebuhr and its peculiar movement towards a dialectical method congruent with an understanding of a God who is active in history. It was over coffee in the kitchen of Max Stackhouse, former professor of social ethics at Andover-Newton Theological School, that I came to a critical awareness of the shaping influence of Niebuhr on cultural issues in contemporary society. I subsequently went on to do a doctoral dissertation in Niebuhr's ethico-theological thought.

In Niebuhr's conceptual framework, I uncovered and came to appreciate much of what he had to say about the dialectics of social struggle, the ironies of history, the sinful thirst for power among human collectivities, and the sovereignty of God's grace over creation—all came together and struck a responsive chord in my own understanding of ethics and theology. Naturally, I approach the shaping influence of Niebuhr's theology and ethics from the boundaries of the black condition and the situation of racism in America. I pondered again and again the existential question, "What is the significance of Niebuhr's ethical thought for someone working within an Afrocentric framework?" Niebuhr's pragmatic relevance for me lies in the fact that one's ethical framework need not be a monolithic methodology or a fixed system of what is "politically correct for all ethnic groups in society." It is not a formal system of ethics rooted in rationalism or idealism, but rather in the crucibles of realism and prophetic witness in the Christian moral life. It seems to me that a basic contribution of Niebuhr's ethical approach to the problem of "race relations" in America centers around his radical orientation toward the world, his positive appraisal of coercion as necessary for oppressed groups, his cultivation of prophetic faith in the search for freedom, the perennial tension in the struggle for truth over falsehood and of integrity over pretension, and the triumph of one's faith in the basic goodness of God in the midst of the tragic contradictions of life.

What we find in Reinhold Niebuhr is a dialectical ethical method, which starts always with the scope of human needs, human powers, and human problems and aspirations, and the integrity of the church's witness to its own mission in the world against the demonic forces of racism, in light of the liberating gospel of Jesus Christ. Theologically considered, it is in the person of Jesus that we find a reality that frees us without letting us go. In the person of Jesus we find an approach to the dilemmas of racism in the wider society that pulls the Christian community of faith toward a vision of human liberation. This does not mean the elimination of ambiguity in the moral life, but rather an invitation to a deeper search for a usable method.

Methologically, it seems to me that the pressing question always before us is simply this: What do we genuinely seek in an ethical method as we reluctently stare at the treacherous mountain of racism in our world today? As a Christian realist, for instance, Reinhold Niebuhr was politically and ethically stubborn in his blistering critique of the assumed doctrine of "inevitable progress" in our democratic republic with respect to ethnic amelioration and the sociocultural assimilation of blacks into the mainstream of American life. Niebuhr wrote:

> The progress of the Negro race...is retarded by the inclination of many...educated Negroes to strive for identification and assimilation with the more privileged white race and to minimize their relation to a subject race as much as possible.[25]

While recent political and social events in our global community may bear witness to the fact of our cultural and religious pluralism, the actual achievement of diversity is not a simple possibility. The apparent goal of many ethnic minorities in our country may not be, necessarily, to become more and more "American"—that is, a "like-us mentality"—but rather to reap the benefits of democratic reform, social justice, and economic parity so that human life can be made more human. Methodologically, the goal is not the old liberal nineteenth-century pseudo-enlightenment notion of a "melting pot"

---

[25]Reinhold Niebuhr, *Moral Man and Immoral Society* (New York: Charles Scribner's Sons, 1932), p. 274.

society where cultural differences are eradicated and swallowed up, but rather the transcultural vision of the "beloved community" where differences are accepted and affirmed.

Moreover, what we search for in an ethical method, I think, is not a pot of gold at the end of the rainbow but the "rainbow itself," as the *summum bonum*, the highest good of our common striving! What we search for, without theological compensation or apology, is truth: the truth of the gospel of Jesus Christ, the truth legitimated through the crucible of our own ethnic histories, and the truth reflected in the integrity of one's own experience and "story of faith."

Less apparent to some and more evident to others, what the human spirit searches for is the "gray thread of diversity-in-unity." For example, the social thought of Carter G. Woodson and Reinhold Niebuhr is indicative of the "gray thread" metaphor, which may encourage us to look more honestly at the mountain of racism in contemporary society.

Who is this man called Carter G. Woodson? Well, to ask a question implies reflection upon that question. Carter G. Woodson is the revered father of "black history." As a historian and scholar of the first rank, Woodson held the conviction that black history is American history; that the true history of the African American had been tragically distorted and demoralized by white racism and the brainwashing techniques of white scholars and public institutions, and thereby relegated to the false status of "inferiority" in the dominant host culture. Intellectually considered, Carter G. Woodson set out to recover and to restore the significant social, moral, religious, and scientific contributions that people of African descent have made to Western civilization and the world.

It is interesting to note that Carter G. Woodson started the movement we now know as "Black History Month" back in the late 1920s, through the organization then known as the Association for the Study of Negro Life and History. Another important clue in regard to the metaphor "a gray thread of diversity-in-unity" stems from the fact that Woodson was a contemporary of Reinhold Niebuhr in the chilling decade of the '30s, with the publication of the classic work *Mis-education of the Negro* in 1933. Some will recall that the previous year, 1932, was a watershed experience in the social thought of Reinhold Niebuhr, with the publication of his most enduring and controversial work, *Moral Man and Immoral Society*. From the viewpoint of comparative social analysis, what is most profound in both volumes is the lifting up of an intercultural hermeneutic, which seeks to unmask the tragic plight of the African American in his search for survival, freedom and dignity in a society not fully of his own making.

The peculiar legacy of chattel slavery and the ironies of American history converged upon the black community, stripped black people of a sense of "cultural memory" and linguistic heritage, and distorted our sense of self-worth. Here I think that Woodson rightly calls this racist phenomenon "the mis-education of the Negro." By contrast, Reinhold Niebuhr tended to use the Marxist method of social analysis and referred to the "inordinate power" and ethical attitudes of the privileged classes over the masses or proletarian classes. Concerning this problem of mis-education, identity and racial oppression, Woodson made the following assertion in 1933:

> The education of the Negro then must be carefully directed lest the race may waste time trying to do the impossible. Lead the Negro to believe this and thus control his thinking. If you can thereby determine what he will think, you will not need to worry about what he will do. You will not have to tell him to go to the back door. He will go without being told; and if there is no back door he will have one cut for his special benefit.[26]

Comparatively speaking, Reinhold Niebuhr perhaps anticipated but could not fully articulate a compassionate ethic of liberation relevant to the dialectics of the black condition in the dominant culture of the 1930s and early 1940s—a period of history marred by racial bigotry, suffering, the horror of the Holocaust, and the lynchings of blacks on the part of the Ku Klux Klan—all of these atrocities symbolize shame and a failure of conscience in our modern global community. Concerning the dilemmas of social struggle for emancipation, Niebuhr wrote in 1932:

---

[26]Carter G. Woodson, *Mis-education of the Negro* (Washington, D.C.: The Associated Publishers, 1933), p. 192.

The emancipation of the Negro race in America probably waits upon the adequate development of this kind of social and political strategy. It is hopeless for the Negro to expect complete emancipation from the menial social and economic position into which the white man has forced him, merely by trusting in the "moral sense" of the white race. It is equally hopeless to attempt emancipation through violent rebellion.[27]

Let us now make a few summary comments on the importance of pluralism and inclusivity in our churches and society as we contemplate the meaning of the "gray thread of diversity." First, it is a glimpse into the obvious to suggest that the gray thread of diversity is not a simple possibility for modern-day Christians to achieve against the backdrop of an Anglo-Saxon people strongly anchored in nineteenth-century rationalism, Protestant liberalism, and German pietism. Second, the gray thread of diversity, as symbolized in the social thought of Woodson and Niebuhr, is not a simple possibility, also because, ironically, we are more alike than we are different; yet the reality of "difference" per se, is both a source of moral strength and conflict, of trust and distrust, of pain and promise. In short, the gray thread of diversity is not a simple possibility because the Macedonian call for justice today, on the part of people of color, may require more than what the dominant power structure in America is willing to give, and more than what the hurting ones can any longer take. Hence, we need an ethical method that reflects this bipolar tension and cultural paradox.

Toward a Method of Covenant-Harambee

From a comparative perspective, the African concept of harambee bears affinity to the Hebraic-Christian notion of covenant. As an analytic construct to better understand the phenomenon of racism in church and society, I submit that it is imperative that we examine both concepts more closely as they shed light upon the complex and dynamic issue of ethnicity and Christian faith in a predominantly white racist society. A closer look reveals that these two elements, *harambee* and *covenant*, are not unconnected parts of historical

---

[27]See Reinhold Niebuhr, pp. 252–256.

reality; but rather, they reflect what Walter Muelder, in his book *Moral Law in Christian Social Ethics* calls "social wholes."[28] In the relational disciplines of ethics and Christian theology, they are paradigmatic lenses that connect two worlds: one white and one black—separate and unequal—as each world agonizes over the possibility of exploring new boundaries and participating more fully in the dance of God among all the multi-cultural and religiously diverse peoples who walk upon this earth. Therefore, it seems to me that a closer look at harambee is in order.

J. Deotis Roberts, in his book *A Black Political Theology*, develops a similar and, indeed, fascinating paradigm, *Ujamma*, as a way to better understand the method of ethical discourse and the painful boundaries of black life in white America. As a theologian of the Christian church, with a keen knowledge of the dialectics of black religious experience, Roberts describes the concept of Ujamma as "togetherness" and "familyhood."[29] Then he goes on to assert its relevance for the Christian church in the wider society by accentuating the principle of radical love as revealed in Jesus Christ. Roberts writes:

> Love as Jesus understood it is an urge for social cooperation in which the cooperating parties treat each other as persons. The welfare of the individual is furthered by the cooperation of all those who are members of the group. In order for an individual to be personal, he must act from within some group. Individuals are persons in society. The church as a fellowship should provide the climate for the flowering of that which is most truly personal as well as the manifestation of genuine community.[30]

In the first place, the basic idea of *harambee*, in the traditional cultural patterns of African society, has come to mean something very profound: it is a symbol of the church not only for "unity," but far more as a normative-redemptive trumpet to sound to a bleeding

[28]Walter G. Muelder, *Moral Law in Christian Social Ethics* (Richmond, Virginia: John Knox Press, 1966), p. 23.
[29]J. Deotis Roberts, *A Black Political Theology* (Philadelphia: Westminster Press, 1974), p. 166.
[30]Ibid., p. 166.

world, "either we hang together in the struggle against racism and European imperialism or we just hang!" The dynamic thing about *harambee* is that it calls Christians from every walk of life—from diverse political, social, and economic backgrounds—to see the church as one body: as a community that lives and suffers together, hopes and dreams together, as a community of faith and action, and as a community of moral discourse summoned by God to bear prophetic witness in our time.

Harambee, in short, is descriptive of the suffering love of Jesus going to bat for the groaning of all creation *together*, so that none may be lost and all may experience the triumphant power of God's kingdom of righteousness and reconciling grace throughout the land. Even though the hounds of hell may spread their "dirty tracks" of division, racial hatred, and fear, the moral agents of harambee can take the high ground and begin to spread their "redeeming tracks" of compassion, justice, and oneness.

In the second place, a key element in our discussion of the search for an ethical method to combat racism, is covenant. The idea of covenant per se, as an informing method ethical discourse in the church's life and faith, is nothing new. Indeed, it is an old concept. There are varieties of covenant: in the modern world, we often speak or hear of covenants between nations, between states, between states and representatives of states, between kings and their subjects, between a military leader and his other soldiers, between individuals and social groups, between husband and wife, between human beings and animals; and also we hear of covenants with death and covenants with life. The list goes on and on.

So, then, the idea itself is far from new. Etymologically, the term *covenant* is derived from the Hebrew word *berith.* The original meaning of the Hebrew *berith* is not "agreement or settlement between two parties," as commonly argued. *Berith* implies first and foremost the notion of "imposition" or "obligation," as might be implied in such phrases as "bond of faith," "strong persistent bond," "to fasten the bonds." Thus, we find that the *berith* is commanded by God (*tsivvah beritho*, he has commanded his covenant). Analytically, the Greek terms for covenant, *harmonia* and *synthesia*, also express pulling together. Comparatively, it is important to note in our critical discussion of racism in church and society that these two elements, *harambee* and *covenant,* combined together constitute a contextual methodology. As Paul Lehmann's methodological orientation suggested, Christian ethics, per se, needs to be developed in context. Theoretically, we must keep in mind, for instance, that *ethics* is behavior according to reason. *Morality* is behavior according to custom. Given the entrenched situation of racism in America, this means that our "customs" must change, if we are to have a future as a multicultural and multiracial church.

Hence, in our agonizing search for a usable ethical method, we arrive at the juncture of naming our discourse: the paradigm of *covenant-harambee.* The methodological paradigm of *covenant-harambee* can empower the oppressed and marginalized people to organically move from rage to reason, from speculative reason to moral rhythm, from fear to faith, from humiliation to hope, and from failure to freedom as we continue to grapple with the perplexing dilemmas of racism in both church and society. For example, the dynamism of this persistent moral struggle for freedom and human dignity on the part of oppressed blacks and other minorities in America is reflected in the song "Ain't Gonna Let Nobody Turn Me 'Round", which was introduced to the civil rights movement in Albany, Georgia, by Ralph Abernathy during the summer of 1962. If we open our hearts, the rhythmic flow implicit in the paradigm of *covenant-harambee* can touch and change human lives as we climb up the mountain of racism to get a glimpse of "freedom land." The song says:

> Ain't gonna let nobody turn me 'round,
> turn me 'round, turn me 'round,
> Ain't gonna let nobody turn me 'round,
> I'm gonna keep on a walkin', keep on a talkin',
> Marching up to freedom land.

> Ain't gonna let segregation turn me 'round,
> turn me 'round, turn me 'round,
> Ain't gonna let segregation turn me 'round,
> I'm gonna keep on a walkin', keep on a talkin',
> Marching up to freedom land.

Ain't gonna let no jailhouse turn me 'round,
turn me 'round, turn me 'round,
Ain't gonna let no jailhouse turn me 'round,
I'm gonna keep on a walkin', keep on a talkin',
Marching up to freedom land.

Ain't gonna let no injunction turn me 'round,
turn me 'round, turn me 'round,
Ain't gonna let no injunction turn me 'round,
I'm gonna keep on a walkin', keep on a talkin',
Marching up to freedom land.[31]

Here the social context for moral struggle on the part of oppressed blacks—with its eschatological affirmation, "ain't gonna let nobody turn me 'round"—is a powerful modern metaphor of the biblical story of the exodus. For example, the ethical method of covenant shapes the way we think about the character of the Christian moral life and how we understand the drama of God's mighty deeds in history. The exodus story was the decisive event in Israel's history, one describing God's liberation of the Israelites—who were once slaves in Egypt—from the yoke of bondage. Concretely, I suspect, therefore, that in the ethical method of covenant, we must mark, symbolically, one of the critical tensions in understanding the problem of racism in contemporary society, namely: the tension between *suffering* and *hope*.

In the exodus story, we recalled how Yahweh heard the sobbing cries and throbbing hearts of the people of Israel and delivered them with a mighty hand of grace and righteousness. As scripture teaches us: God "heard their groaning, and God remembered his covenant with Abraham, Isaac, and Jacob; God looked upon the Israelites, and God took notice of them" (Exod. 2:24–25). By the same token, we may observe that blacks and other oppressed peoples in the civil rights movement of the sixties seemed to take the high road of *hope* by unabashedly proclaiming to the movers and shakers of a racist society: "I'm gonna keep on a walkin', keep on a talkin', marching

---

[31] Thomas R. Frazier, ed., *Afro-American History* (Chicago: Dorsey Press, 1988), pp. 370–371.

up to freedom land!" Here it seems that what emerges from the social context of the sixties civil rights era is a *Camelot moment*, where the notion of covenant and the spirit of harambee may come together as a composite image for a new ethical method by which the ethically sensitive Christian may struggle in climbing the treacherous mountain of racism in America. While there are, undoubtedly, many scholarly voices in the field of Christian social ethics in regard to methods and procedures in contemporary society, I feel some deep passion about the proposal to link, methodologically, the organic concepts of "covenant" and "harambee," as a way to interpret and fashion a reasonable response to the perennial problem of racism in our culture.

Moreover, the many and varied ways by which sensitive scholars and faithful teachers of the church do ethics can, in fact, lead to a composite image of an ethical method that holds promise for us in the struggle to overcome the mountain of racism in American society. As we have already observed in our analysis, the critical writings of Rauschenbusch, Buber, Lehmann, and Niebuhr are highly suggestive in the *indicative* sense of revealing certain theological understandings and ethical assumptions that do shed light, historically, upon the phenomenon of racism. However, it is interesting to note—as African American religious scholars have rightly pointed out—that these allegedly "universal" theological understandings and moral claims about God, church, community, and the human person are indeed necessary, but not sufficient.

Concretely speaking, the dominant theological understandings and ethical assumptions about the good, right, and fitting thing to do—however noble and virtuous in theory—are deeply embedded in the Eurocentric traditions of culture and church life that perpetuate, rather than *dismantle* the scourge of racism. Assuming that we are committed to becoming a part of the solution, we are still faced with the shameful fact that Anglo-American Christians are part of the *problem.* This is not a matter of "dumping guilt"—God only knows that there is enough guilt in each of us to go around the world a thousand times over! Existentially, the salty question is this: Can the moral agent critically move from a largely rationalistic posture of the "head-only" to a synergistic posture, tacitly and explicily embodied in the idea of harambee, of both "head and heart" in the search for the beloved community beyond the mountain of racism? Accordingly, I propose, in terms of its symbiotic function, a style of ethical discourse of *in-betweenness*, which seeks to incorporate certain norms, paradigms, and typologies from Euro-American ethics that could possibly eliminate racism—in collaboration with certain patterns of discernment, wisdom and faith from the Afrocentric religio-cultural heritage. In the corpus of African American Christian ethics, I contend that such a composite vision for an ethical method could provide us with a more honest assessment of *where we are*, and perhaps trigger some clues as an image of potentiality of where *we ought to be*. I call this ethical sensibility the organic rhythm of moving from a largely rationalistic mode expressive of the Enlightenment to *harambee*—that is, the understanding of moral agency which is a response of the total personality to the complex problems of human existence. This is an understanding of moral agency based essentially on *relationality* and *hospitality* in human community. Hence, what I am boldly suggesting here is nothing less than an ethical method of *covenant-harambee* as a model for combating racism in our time.

In the corpus of African American Christian ethics, we may further say that the Swahili concept of *harambee* is ethically tied in with the notions of "unity," "kinship," and "community." For example, in traditional African society the moral agent is an individual whose personal identity possesses virtue and standing only in relation to the social reality of the community. At its very core, the reality of individual narrative has worth or moral validation only as a constitutive element of the kinship bond. So, then, as one member of the close family or kinship suffers, *all* suffer. By the same token, when one person of the kinship rejoices over the goodness of God, or some fortune, the whole village is inevitably blessed!

The implications of a *covenant-harambee* method of ethical discourse for combating racism are enormously important. For example, racism is a messy situation in America; but we all are *in* the "mess," and victimized by the mess together: whether we are red, yellow, black or white. Of course, I am quick to acknowledge that some are more victimized *by* the "mess," while others benefit *from* the "mess." Notwithstanding, the *conditio sine qua non* is that no one ethnic group operating alone can negate—entirely—the mess we're in. Fundamentally, there is a craving, a restless search in the human spirit for a common moral discourse. Methodologically, I think that the perennial craving for the ethical is a craving for a certain bond of unity and a sense of "hospitality" beyond the mountain of racism. Meanwhile, we must here struggle with a sense of greater clarity on the concept of kinship itself. John Mbiti expresses well this covenant-harambee model:

Moral Decision Making: Seven-Stage Model

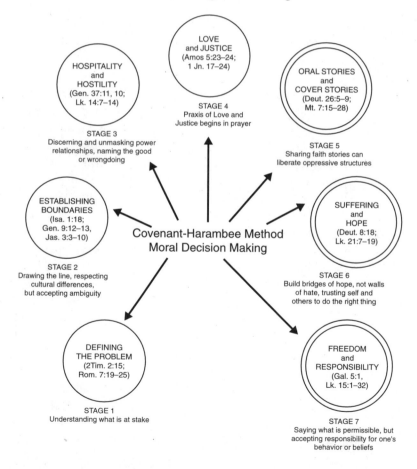

LOVE
and JUSTICE
(Amos 5:23–24;
1 Jn. 17–24)

STAGE 4
Praxis of Love and
Justice begins in prayer

HOSPITALITY
and
HOSTILITY
(Gen. 37:11, 10;
Lk. 14:7–14)

STAGE 3
Discerning and unmasking power
relationships, naming the good
or wrongdoing

ORAL STORIES
and
COVER STORIES
(Deut. 26:5–9;
Mt. 7:15–28)

STAGE 5
Sharing faith stories can
liberate oppressive structures

ESTABLISHING
BOUNDARIES
(Isa. 1:18;
Gen. 9:12–13,
Jas. 3:3–10)

STAGE 2
Drawing the line, respecting
cultural differences,
but accepting ambiguity

Covenant-Harambee Method
Moral Decision Making

SUFFERING
and
HOPE
(Deut. 8:18;
Lk. 21:7–19)

STAGE 6
Build bridges of hope, not walls
of hate, trusting self and
others to do the right thing

DEFINING
THE PROBLEM
(2Tim. 2:15;
Rom. 7:19–25)

STAGE 1
Understanding what is at stake

FREEDOM
and
RESPONSIBILITY
(Gal. 5:1,
Lk. 15:1–32)

STAGE 7
Saying what is permissible, but
accepting responsibility for one's
behavior or beliefs

Kinship is reckoned through blood and betrothal (engagement and marriage). It is kinship which controls social relationships between people in a given community: it governs marital customs and regulations, it determines the behavior of one individual toward another. Indeed, this sense of kinship binds together the entire life of the "bride," and is even extended to cover animals, plants and nonliving objects through the "totemic" system. Almost all the concepts connected with human relationship can be understood and interpreted through the kinship system. This it is which largely governs the behavior, thinking and whole life of the individual in the society of which he is a member.[32]

It seems to me that in our perennial discussion on the quest for an ethical method for moral decision making, the African notion of "kinship" can function as a normative source for understanding the viability and construction of a covenant-harambee model for moral decision making. I submit that it is not a perfect model for struggling with the ultimate questions of truth, freedom, responsibility, meaning, and the quest for genuine identity in the difficult places of ministry in our global community. However, it may serve as a different springboard for the ethically sensitive reader. But I think, all things being equal—which they never are, the primary reason we must struggle so unrelentingly with the question of ethical method—especially in the context of the black religious experience in America—is that there is not a coherent principle of internal self-criticism which enables the moral agent to deal creatively with the cultural ambiguities, religious polarities, and problematic tensions of black life. Thus the ethical method of covenant-harambee represents a paradigm shift and important new starting point. In the following typology, we may consider the orientational aspects of this method as a way to broaden our understanding of the destructive force of racism in the United States.

An interpretive analysis that is ethically self-critical of the difficult problem of racism in church and society can be illustrated as we examine the stages of moral decision making implicit in the covenant-

---

[32]John S. Mbiti, *African Religions and Philosophies* (New York: Anchor Books, 1970), p. 135.

harambee method. From a conceptual frame of reference, the "stages" of moral reasoning regarding critical issues at stake are perceived to be dynamic and relational rather than static and passive. In our perennial struggle to make sense out of the situation of racism in white America in light of the Christian faith, the proposed alternative methodology of covenant-harambee holds the viewpoint that these developmental stages share a symbiotic relationship. In a broad sense the term "symbiosis" presupposes an organic link or nexus among the various stages of decision making that challenges the ethically sensitive Christian to be conceptually clear about the critical problem of racism in the United States. Thus the reader will observe that in so-called Stage One (defining the problem), the moral agent comes face-to-face with the challenge of disciplined study to determine "what is at stake" in climbing the treacherous mountain of racism in our culture. Figuratively, I cannot fully know, in the totality of my being as a child of God, the critical issues at stake on the question of racism without *first* "looking at," in the words of the pop-music superstar Michael Jackson, "The Man in the Mirror"! More succinctly, the Pauline ethic of the early church simply reminds us of a profound truth in our description of Stage One, namely: "Do your best to present yourself to God as one approved by him, a worker who has no need to be ashamed, rightly explaining the word of truth." (2 Tim 2:15, NRSV).

I suspect that Stage Two is exceedingly important for the moral agent in one's reflections on the problematic "race and religion" in American culture, because it attempts to set before the doorsteps the cruciality of "establishing moral boundaries." Analytically, Stage Two in our covenant-harambee method seeks to describe the sort of attitudes, sentiments, and activities that are *permissible* in a multicultural and multiracial church. For example, I recently conducted a workshop on "Race and Religion" for a cluster of local congregations in St. Louis, Missouri, largely made up of Anglo-American Christians. I vividly recall—after two successful evening seminars as people began to feel more comfortable with the topic—a nice older Anglo-American Christian woman came up to me and said: "You know, you're the first colored seminary professor that I had a workshop with on the academic study of race and religion...that didn't lay a guilt trip on me about how bad white people are…People are just people and I don't see color." Surely this woman was sincere and expressed a legitimate concern for seeing, ultimately, all people as just people—as children of God. After we talked further, I boldly affirmed her religious conviction and moral claim of the importance of the universal inclusivity of all humanity. But I hastened to add and to remind her—in the spirit of speaking the truth-in-love—that the term "colored seminary professor" needed a bit of upgrading; and that it was morally and culturally "permissible" to actually affirm or "see" *color*. In short, with this particular incident it seemed as though a light went off in this nice woman's head, since she apparently had not thought about it that way before! If one wants to probe further into Stage Two on the value of establishing "permissible" moral boundaries, this reality-constructing story may illustrate a small step on the road toward better understanding as partners in covenant-relationship with God.

Moreover, the elements of Stage Three, *hospitality or hostility*, in our covenant-harambee method of moral reasoning seek to describe two contrasting life forces. Theoretically, we may say here that the moral agent is always confronted with the faith challenge of testing whether existing boundaries between blacks and whites, Haitians and Asians, and other people of color in our society are, in fact, hostile or friendly. It would seem to me that the individual who is concerned with the dynamics of moral decision making is compelled to raise certain critical questions, namely: What kinds of acts reflect either the spirit of "hospitality" or the burden of "hostility" in the context of ethnic relations in America? What values enhance or contribute to the spirit of hospitality in human community? How can the church genuinely participate as a community of moral discourse on the question of racism and "pulling down walls of hostility" when for some the proverbial 11:00 Sunday worship hour is still the most segregated hour in American life? These are a few of the issues one may face at Stage Three in our description of a covenant-harambee method for addressing the perennial dilemmas of race and religion in our society.

In our conceptual chart, the dynamic elements of "love and justice" comprise Stage Four in our covenant-harambee method of moral discourse. For ethnic relations in America the critical writings of Reinhold Niebuhr remind us that neither love nor justice is a simple possibility for the church in American culture. The norm of love is enormously important in our covenant-harambee method of moral decision making. In a fragmented society broken by the triadic evils of racism, sexism, and classism, the language of love must be held in tension with the demands for justice on the part of marginalized oppressed peoples in the global community. The norm of love in the conceptual chart is viewed to be "the law of life," to use the language of Reinhold Niebuhr. The norm of "love," therefore, refers to the possibility of human equality and mutuality under the perennial conditions of racism and oppression in America. As ethically sensitive Christians, the real danger for us, according to Niebuhr, is the tendency to reduce the principle of love to some kind of sentimentalism in church and society. While the ethical ideal of love may stand as an ultimate criterion in ethnic relations, it can never be used as a noble substitute for concrete justice in society— where issues of racial bigotry, power, and greed are always at stake. Hence, our current method for moral decision making on matters of race and religion sees justice as an indispensable norm of the social order.

As for a critical theory of ethnic relations, I agree with Niebuhr that love and justice must remain in creative tension. Love and justice are paradoxical. In this sense, our covenant-harambee method of moral discourse means that each child of God should get his or her "just due"; that true love can never negate justice at the bargaining table of power and enlightened self-interest in our American sociocultural system. It seems to me that the notion of justice in our chart refers to the degree of love that can be achieved under the perennial pressures of racism, classism, and conflicting claims of social groups. Thus I contend methodologically that justice is a *corrective norm* in human society, while love is an *ultimate norm* that holds all human beings accountable for the virtues and vices of historical existence.

Summarily, the creative tensions inherent in Stage Four of our model for critical decision are neatly reflected in the following ethical dictums by Reinhold Niebuhr: "Any justice which is only justice soon degenerates into something less than justice. It must be saved by something which is more than justice."[33]

The identifying characteristics of Stage Five (oral stories and cover stories) seem to vary from one situation to another. However, I would like to suggest to the reader some distinctive contrasting motifs. First, there is in human community the characteristic motif of *orality*, as a source for moral decision making. For example, the first of covenant-harambee is rooted in oral culture, which takes the form of storytelling. Storytelling puts the *true* claims of biblical faith in tension with the *false claims* of earthly powers, which I call or refer to in our ethical method as "cover stories." Hence, we may define a "cover story" in our chart as a story of self-deceit, falsehood, and death. An "oral story" may be defined as life-giving; a story of self-integrity, freedom, and faith in the moral struggle to pursue the truth and meaning of human existence. Second, we may observe that for Christians the oral stories are nurtured by what we remember as a people of God. Historical memory is therefore a very important aspect of existential testimony and being in the world, as moral agents engaged in critical decision making. A third characteristic motif of *orality* is the recognition that people with a shared memory of oppression and moral struggle think in relationships.[34] For example, a covenant-harambee method of moral decision making seems to use "relationships" as a lens through which to view and to remember what the God of biblical faith can do for a people acquainted with oppression and injustice. Hence, the upshot of *orality* means that scripture is remembered and read differently through the eyes of those who are oppressed by racist structures in society. For example, listen for the sounds of a new method of liberation, which I call covenant-harambee, as implicitly disclosed in God's righteous hand of deliverance of the Hebrews from the yoke of bondage:

> When the Egyptians treated us harshly and afflicted us, by imposing hard labor on us, we cried to the LORD, the God of our ancestors; the LORD heard our voice and saw our affliction, our

---

[33]See Reinhold Niebuhr, p. 258.

[34]Tex Sample, *Ministry in an Oral Culture: Living with Will Rogers, Uncle Remus, and Minnie Pearl* (Louisville: Westminster/John Knox Press, 1994), p. 5.

toil, and our oppression. The LORD brought us out of Egypt with a mighty hand and an outstretched arm, with a terrifying display of power, and with signs and wonders; and he brought us into this place and gave us this land, a land flowing with milk and honey. (Deut 26:6–9)

In our discussion of the orientational aspects of a covenant-harambee method for moral decision making, we come now to Stage Six (Suffering and Hope). Here the moral agent is primarily concerned with a critical awareness of the organic interface of suffering and hope as perennial themes in the drama of biblical faith. The process of critical awareness implies on the political level of ethical discourse and decision making that the people of God must get involved in progressive community projects, which can provide a logical alternative to the assumed posture of inferiority in regard to non-whites in the wider society. It is politically axiomatic to say that marginalized people living in America are victimized by the cruel hand of poverty, racism, and involuntary suffering. What is needed at this Sixth Stage of moral decision making is nothing less than a bold program of community action, sufficiently capable of generating real attitudinal and sociopolitical change in the moral fabric of how Anglo-American Christians relate to people of color. In short, the motif or element of "hope" in our orientational chart becomes more than just a word as the community of faith works toward genuine structural change—as the Christian believer or moral agent says NO to white racism in all its forms. Put another way, what is needed at this Sixth Stage of moral decision-making is for the victims of injustice and racism to see clearly see that they need not remain victims: in a nutshell, *political education for systemic change is a viable alternative to involuntary suffering in a racist society.*

Finally, the moral agent is compelled to ponder, in Stage Seven, the notion that freedom and responsibility belong together in our struggle with the deep issues of life in both church and society. For example, the awakening of some whites to their "white male privilege" in American society must be an aim or goal of an alternative ethical method. I suspect that such an awakening of white male privilege is one of the most difficult and unresolved dilemmas in the

general theory of methodology of Christian social ethics in contemporary society. To be sure, I think that the aim here must be one
of conscientization and constructive dialogue rather than "rock
throwing" and moralistic blame for the apparently deep chasms of
fear and rivers of mistrust that exist between whites and blacks,
Latinos, Asians, Native Americans and other people of color in our
multi-cultural and multiracial society. Therefore, the spirit of covenant-harambee requires a methodological shift of ethical discourse
that enhances a sense of freedom without abandoning the principle
of responsibility for our attitudes, sentiments, and conduct in a civil
society.

3

Racism and Niggerism: Are They First Cousins?

Hope has two beautiful daughters. Their names are anger and
courage: anger at the way things are, and courage to see that they do
not remain the way they are.

—*Augustine*

Introduction

Symbolically, the presence of "hope" is the *élan vitale* that enables
morally sensitive Christians to grapple with the dilemmas of racism and
niggerism—the use of the word "nigger" to describe African Americans—in our time. In our discussion so far we have already suggested
that the covenant-harambee model is an important paradigm for understanding the complexities of the black religious experience in
America. In one sense, the covenant-harambee model of ethical discourse must proceed from the assumption, I think, that the wellness or
psychic health of the whole community and the nation necessarily
involves a strong sense of self-responsibility. Accordingly, we must now

move analytically in our discussion to the problems of niggerism in ghetto life.

For the Afrocentric moral agent, this is not an easy ethical concern to raise for at least two pragmatic reasons. First, there is always the danger or risk of misinterpretation and abuse on the part of the oppressor of blacks and other people of color—in regard to the irrational tendency to place "niggerism" and racism on an *even* par. Historically considered, that would be a terrible mistake, due in part to our critical understanding of racism in America as consisting of the triadic elements of prejudice, power, and privilege. Second, there is the perceived sentiment or "feeling" in certain quarters of black America that the word "nigger" has become a necessary term of *endearment*, since the prevailing values and social structure of the dominant Euro-American culture have denied blacks and other minorities their basic human rights and self-worth. Thus, there is a thick cloud of ambiguity around the term "nigger" in the parlance of "hip-hop" black culture and social thought.

Problematic Words and Shades of Ambiguity

Linguistically considered, words are like powerful works of art—they connote different shades of meaning, depending upon the user and the context. Of course the use of the term "nigger"—linguistically and culturally—falls within a kinetic vineyard of shifting boundaries and meanings. Thus the explosive term "nigger" means many things to different people—contingent upon what is in the user's head and heart at a given moment in time, discarding or affirming one's self-esteem at the conflicted junctures of failure and faith, of oppression and liberation, and of despair and hope in the lived world of experience.

It seems to me that within the sociocultural context of racism in America, many morally concerned people don't know what to do, with this baffling word "nigger." Is it a blessing in disguise for the victimized? Or is it an unforgivable curse of Anglo-Saxon colonialism that refuses to die on the new frontier of American democracy? For Christians of conscience, is it ever morally right or permissible to use the term "nigger"? Should African Americans ever use the term "nigger" to each other as an affectionate expression of endearment? I think that it is enormously important for us as people of faith and conscience to raise these salty questions and issues. I suspect that the sort of response we come up with will undoubtedly impact the identity and shape of ethnic relations in the church of the twenty-first century. To shed some initial light and understanding conceptually upon this critical dilemma in the use of certain pejorative words, Geneva Smitherman's work *Black Talk: Words and Phrases from the Hood to the Amen Corner* seems to be relevant in our ethical discussion. Here concerning the term "nigga," she writes:

> Used with a variety of meanings, ranging from positive to negative to neutral. 1) "She my main nigga," that is, She is my close friend, my back-up. 2) "Now that Brotha, see, he ain like them ol e-lights, he real, he is a shonuff nigga," i.e., He is culturally Black and rooted in Blackness and the African American Experience. 3) "That party was live; it was wall-to-wall niggas there," a generic, neutral use of the word, meaning simply that many African Americans were present at the party. 4) "Guess we ain gon be seein too much of girlfriend no mo since she got herself a new nigga," African American women's neutral/generic term for a Black man, here meaning simply that the woman in question has a new boyfriend.[1]

In a different manner, we may observe how Smitherman links historically the term "nigga" with racist patterns of oppression and injustice suffered by African Americans in the wider culture. She emphatically asserts:

> When used by whites, nigga has historically been used in a negative sense, as a racial epithet, to CALL an African person outa they name—and usually pronounced "nigger," not nigga.

---

[1]Geneva Smitherman, *Black Talk: Words and Phrases from the Hood to the Amen Corner* (New York: Houghton Mifflin Co., 1994), p. 167. In the critical discussion and debate over the public usage of the term "nigga," it is interesting to observe that the motivation for this current book grew out of a literary project in the 1970s, dealing with the language of *ebonics*. Here Smitherman produced a volume, *Talklin and Testifying: The Language of Black America*, which was subsequently published by Houghton Mufflin in 1977. In both volumes, the author demonstrates great skill and acumen in addressing the variety and shades of meanings that black folk give to certain words and cultural idioms, as a result of living in a racist society.

However, the frequent use of nigga in Rap Music, on "Def Comedy Jam," and throughout Black Culture generally, where the word takes on meanings other than the historical negative, has created a linguistic dilemma in the crossover world and in the African American community. Widespread controversy rages about the use of the term—and about whether or not whites can have license to use THE N-word with the many different meanings that Blacks give to it.[2]

In any event, we must be aware, ethically, of the variety of meanings, shapes of interpretation, and the peculiar cultural idioms which may impact how the user perceives and internalizes the word "nigga." Be that as it may, I simply think that the "negatives" outweigh the "positives."

While my uneasiness about usage of this racial epithet may merit a word of caution, I think that a viable model of covenant-harambee demands that we seek new ways of responding to an "old dilemma" within the church and wider society, namely, what "language" or "catchword" seems appropriate in describing a person of African descent? In terms of the covenant-harambee orientation, I think that we have implicit in this model of ethical discourse a place for internal self-criticism about what is right and wrong in the use of certain explosive and inflammatory language such as "nigger." Here I think that a critical glance at the history of black-white relations in America may provide us with a clue to the problematic usage of the term "nigger."

---

[2]Ibid., pp. 167–168. Critical studies in the areas of linguistics and philosophical ethics seem to suggest that while the widespread controversy continues to rage over the use of the term "nigga," an equally intriguing controversy is emerging in regard to the word "nigger." For example, some African-centered folk have real problems with the hip-hop use of the term "wigger"— which has emerged in the counter-cultural movement to mean literally "white nigger." Linguistically, it presumably applies to a European American who affectionately identifies with the prevailing values, sentiments, and social traditions of black culture in the United States. Accordingly, Geneva Smitherman describes the word *wigger* or *wigga* as "an emerging positive term for white youth who identify with Hip Hop, Rap, and other aspects of African American culture. Throughout U. S. history, there have always been *wiggas*, and writer Norman Mailer dubbed them 'white Negroes.' Their numbers are…larger today than in previous generations because of the exposure to African American culture made possible by television" (p. 237).

Colonial Snapshots from History

As we struggle for more education and enlightenment in the future, I believe that the first right of a people who want to be free is the right to define one's own reality. For example, Malcolm X reminded this generation of young adults that education is our passport to the future, for tomorrow belongs to the people who prepare for it today. Accordingly, the covenant-harambee model of ethical discourse insists that we have more education about the dangers of both racism *and* niggerism, if we are to avoid the slippery pitfall of what Carter G. Woodson called the "mis-education" of African Americans. Ethically, we may logically ask, "What is the relation of racism and niggerism in American history?" Well, in my own agony and existential struggle with this question, I have concluded that they are not blood brothers, but "first cousins" in a long family feud, generated by centuries of European imperialism and colonialism and the subsequent domination of white over black, which took its initial economic roots in the establishment of a form of slavery in Jamestown, Virginia, in 1619.[3] According to C. Eric Lincoln, John Hope Franklin, Benjamin Quarles, and other noted American historians, the term "nigger" was undoubtedly used to describe the human cargo as a Dutch frigate attacked a vessel from Portugal and took twenty African slaves. Ironically, in the routine of that day in

---

[3]Vincent Harding, *There Is a River: The Black Struggle for Freedom in America* (New York: Harcourt Brace Jovanovich, 1981), pp. 26–50. Here the author points out that in the Southern colonies — of which Virginia and South Carolina were integral — the legal category of "slave" had not been clearly defined by the colonizers. But what was clear in the dominant culture of Jamestown was the distinctively bold appearance of the African in skin color: he was *black*. Unblemished and starkly black, the African stood out in a crowd — like a solitary red rose in the midst of a garden of ivory; or more realistically discerned, the African's blackness stood out like a defenseless sheep amid a pack of hungry wolves. "The most arresting characteristic of the newly discovered African was his color," says Winthrop Jordan. "Travelers rarely failed to comment upon it; indeed when describing Negroes they…began with complexion and then moved on to dress…and manner." Here I think that the bottom line is that because Englishmen found initially the "natives" of Africa to be so very different from themselves in color and manners, it apparently became easier to call them degrading names such as "niggers" or "coons." Hence, the African's complexion had a powerful impact upon Englishmen's perceptions and worldview. (See Winthop D. Jordan, *White Over Black: American Attitudes Toward the Negro 1550–1812*, Baltimore, Maryland: Penguin Books, Inc., 1968, pp. 4–11.)

late August 1619, the actual landing of the Dutch frigate at Jamestown, with twenty Africans, did not apparently make any immediate impact on the social climate of the colony. But this new racial element had extraordinary consequences. Benjamin Quarles, in his classic book *The Negro in the Making of America*, depicted the whole event this way: "The vessel that sailed into the Chesapeake waters was a privateer, and its coming was as casual and...as unexciting as its consequences were far-reaching."[4]

It is only a glimpse into the obvious to suggest that these first Jamestown Africans—called "negers" by their captors—marked the beginning of the Anglo-Saxon African American experience in the "new" world. Notwithstanding, they were not free, but fell into the category of "indentured servants." Rhetorically, we ask, "What is an indentured servant?" Well, to ask a question means to provide a response. The category of indentured servants referred to those persons from any race or ethnic group who had bound themselves to work for their masters for a specified length of time—generally four years—in return for paying the cost of their transportation across the Atlantic.[5]

It is interesting to observe that with the large-scale economic demands for "cheap labor" in colonial America, the status of Africans as "indentured servants" remained for only the first twenty-five years after their coming to Jamestown in 1619. The raw forces of greed and agricultural expansionism in tobacco and rice increased the demand for cheap labor in colonial America. Ironically, the net result was awesomely devastating for the sons and daughters of African descent: "Negro servitude became synonymous with Negro slavery,"[6] to paraphrase Benjamin Quarles. Concerning this uneasy and coercive marriage between indentured servitude and Negro slavery, Quarles writes:

> Bent on large-scale production of tobacco and rice, proprietors found that slavery had marked advantages over servitude. The slave's services were for life, whereas the indentured servant only

---

[4]Benjamin Quarles, *The Negro in the Making of America* (New York: Macmillan Co., 1969), p. 33.
[5]Ibid., p. 34.
[6]Ibid., p. 35.

worked for a time, generally four years. At the end of a servant's period the master had to give him "freedom dues"—clothing, a small sum of money, or a plot of land—an expense never incurred with slaves. The latter, moreover, replaced themselves by breeding, since their offspring belonged to the master. And, as a rule, it was cheaper to feed and clothe a slave than an indentured servant. The increased need for slaves in colonial America came at a time when slavery had become synonymous with Negro. Whites were never slaves.[7]

Perhaps it is noteworthy to observe that the cruel dialectics of racism and colonialism during this period of American history made it easier for white Anglo-Saxon Protestants to call Africans "negers"— i.e., being passionately regarded by their captors as subhuman and inferior: less intelligent, less moral, less hardworking, less patriotic, and less theological, without "proper" religion and culture. Thus the "seasoning" process for the making of a "nigger" has its origins in the long shadows of colonialism, British economic expansionism, and the hegemonic ways by which whites have controlled blacks and others since the early years of the seventeenth century. Parenthetically, it is also interesting to note that there is no historical record, to my knowledge, to validate a view that Africans *first* called each other "niggers," back in their native homeland. For example, they took on noble names from their revered elders and ancestors.

According to John S. Mbiti, in his book *African Religions and Philosophies*, the act of naming children was an important ritual or ceremony in many traditional African societies, often reflecting the time and circumstance of a child's birth.[8] "For example, if the birth occurs during rain," says Mbiti, "the child would be given a name which means 'Rain,' or 'Rainy,' or 'Water'; if the mother is on a journey at the time, the child might be called 'Traveler,' 'Stranger'...'Wanderer'...."[9] In the language of Swahili, names such as Tai, (meaning "Eagle"), Msiter (meaning "Forest"), or Mlima (meaning "Mountain") may be regarded as common in certain

---

[7]Ibid., p. 34.
[8]John S. Mbiti, *African Religions and Philosophies* (New York: Anchor Books, 1970), p. 154.
[9]Ibid., p. 154.

religio-cultural traditions of East Africa. Therefore, it is not insignificant for the moral agent to recognize that nearly all African names reflect some pattern of meaning.

So, then, the name "nigger" came about not from the religio-cultural ethos of traditional African societies; but rather, it came from white Europeans. It emanated apparently from the "seasoning" process of transforming (literally making, like a blacksmith shaping iron tools for hard labor) a "noble warrior" into a "brute slave" on the part of the planter class, who controlled both the land and the labor force. Of course, this whole brutal system of oppression and exploitation had legal status in colonial America and therefore, made it easier for even slaves themselves—at least some—to take on, apparently, the prevailing attitudes, values, and "customary practices" of their white oppressors, not excluding the self-destructive patterns of name-calling such as "coon," "boy," "annie," "darkie," or "nigger." In the labor fields of both Virginia and Maryland, for instance, this whole matter had legal status in colonial America. In the classic work *Roll, Jordan, Roll: The World the Slaves Made*, Eugene D. Genovese asserts:

> The laws of Virginia and Maryland, as well as those of the colonies to the south, increasingly gave masters the widest possible power over the slaves and also, through prohibition of interracial marriage and the general restriction of slave status to nonwhites, codified and simultaneously preached white supremacy. Kenneth Stamp writes: "Thus the master class, for its own purposes, wrote chattel slavery, the caste system, and color prejudice into American custom and law." These earliest, Draconian slave codes served as a model for those adopted by new slave states during the nineteenth century....[10]

In any event, the upshot of this historical scenario is the fact that the term "neger" (as it was called), was a negatively imposed tag that was fastened to the back of Africans, from the beginning, as a way to keep them in their "place." Even now, the *American College Dictionary* defines the terms "Negro" and "Nigger" to be the same:

---

[10]Eugene D. Genovese, *Roll, Jordan, Roll* (New York: Vintage Books, 1976), p. 31.

"As a member of any dark-skinned race." To be sure, there is a certain blanket of nihilism that covers the soul when one tries to explain to an innocent school-age child why some white people call black people "nigger"; and even more profoundly ironic, why some black people call other black people nigger. The civil rights activist Dick Gregory reflects upon this menacing moral dilemma of black-white relations in contemporary American society:

> When you pull up to the school building, you see the cops barricading it and the sheriff says, "Where you going, nigger?" And you say, "I'm going to school." The little kid looks up and says, "Mornin', mister." And the sheriff snaps, "Well, you can't bring that car in here." So you park the car and get out. You tightly grip that little black hand in yours and the inside of your hand is soaking wet with sweat. Not the five-year-old kid's sweat, but your own ....
>
> The next thing you know you are lying in the gutter with that cracker's foot on your chest and a double-barreled shotgun on your throat. And you hear a voice say, "Move, nigger, and I'll blow your brains out." You're terrified but you think how ironic it is that the only time white folks will admit you have brains is when they are talking about what they are going to do to them.[11]

Rap Culture and Niggerology

In our analytic and ethical discourse we shall use, in our current discussion of the wider problem of racism in America, the terms "niggerism" and "niggerology" interchangeably. Comparatively, we may observe that the language of "nigger" is almost like a virus in the air of contemporary black culture. There are very few places you can go, if you are black, where you can be free of the effects of this social virus. Like its first cousin racism, niggerism is dehumanizing and destructive of the moral fabric of the black community. Like sexism, it dehumanizes our women, mothers, and daughters by reducing them to mere objects of sexual gratification and black male

---

[11]Dick Gregory, *Write Me In!* (New York: Bantam Books, 1968), pp. 46–47.

fantasy. Thus niggerism negates the ethical reality of personhood by perverting and transmuting the ethical reality of personhood into the object-reality of the individual as commodity. For example, the destructive force of niggerism seems most acute to me in the so-called "rap culture" of urban America. Consider the following inflammatory lyrics from the artist NWA in the gangsta rap song, "Niggas for Life":

> It's plain to see
> you can't change me,
> 'Cause I'm a be a
> Nigga for life.[12]

A similar form of gangsta rap music, describing a dangerous pattern of black street life in urban America, can be seen in another rapper known as Dr. Dre from his album entitled "The Chronic." The song itself, "Rat-Tat-Tat-Tat," portrays the same image of negativity regarding the term nigga, in the culture of gangsta rap. The lyrics read:

> Rat-Tat-Tat-Tat
> tit-tit-tat like that;
> (and I) never hesitate
> to put a nigga on
> his back![13]

---

[12]See the record album "Niggaz 4 Life," by the rap group NWA. Here it is important for the writer to point out to that the complex sociopolitical situation of black suffering in white America has in fact, contributed to the variety of meanings associated with the term "nigga." In contrast to NWA, some artists attribute positive elements to the controversial term. For example, *Source* magazine on one occasion described filmmaker Spike Lee and NBA (Phoenix Suns) superstar Charles Barkley as "Nineties Niggers." Ironically constructive, the ethical implication here is that the term "nigga" refers to a rebellious and fearless person, who refuses to accept the conventional values and normative authority of a Eurocentric social system run largely by white males in the United States. In opposition ideologically to "Uncle Tom" athletes and filmmakers, these "Nineties Niggas" are sometimes referred to by writers as "bad niggas," which means—in a moral sense—acting out for the sake of a common good and thereby repudiating vulgar stereotypes of black people in our global society. (Cited in Geneva Smitherman's *Black Talk: Words and Phrases from the Hood to the Amen Corner*), pp. 167–169.

[13]See the song, "Rat-Tat-Tat-Tat," by rap artist Dr. Dre (from album "The Chronic," Death Row Record Company).

It seems to me that such vile, loathsome, and vulgar lyrics offend the moral sensibility of decent human beings—whether they are black or white, rich or poor, old or young, learned or unlearned. There is a sinister element of oppression implicit in the corpus of black suffering and pain of a people deeply burdened by more than 375 years of systemic racism that, in fact, turns in on itself. In the famous words of Jesse Jackson, a Christian humanist and noted civil rights advocate: "Black people in general…and our youth in particular, have turned on each other rather than to each other in love and respect." It is interesting to note that some traditional religious leaders in the black community have referred to this menacing pattern of behavior as rooted in the "crabs-in-the-bucket" mentality. Symbolically, this means that as one individual tries to pull him or herself out of the bucket of despair and degradation, another individual pulls that same person down again. Philosophically we may say that such a pattern of deviant behavior is essentially Sisyphean in character. To be sure, it contributes in our time to the horrors of racism and extreme forms of "niggerology" in urban America. Theologically, the morally honest person is called by God to be not only an antiracist but also an antiniggerologist. By definition, functionally speaking, an antiniggerologist is a moral advocate against the use of the term "nigger" by any ethnic group members—whether black or white—because of its negativity and slave origins in the Americas.

In any event, the self-destructive act, I think, of turning on each other rather than to each other is painfully real in the so-called "gangsta rap music" as epitomized by the group NWA. While resisting the impulse to be moralistic or judgmental, I think I must say passionately that such vulgar lyrics rob the user of a sense of dignity and force the already racially victimized to become burdened with a distorted pattern of dehumanization in the form of racism and *niggerology.* Comparatively, just as there are white people who are in denial about racism, there are black people in denial about niggerism or the uncritical tendency to call each other "my nigger" either affectionately or with malicious disdain! In the jaded tapestry of black culture in America, the proverbial equivalent of the term *nigger* is the word *niggerologist.* Ironically, it is an exceedingly troublesome thought to become a moving target for both the racist and the niggerologist. As I have strongly stated thus far, I am by no means suggesting that both are *equal* in power in the American sociocultural system. Ethically, to make that suggestion on the part of the moral agent would be tantamount to a flight into unreality. However, I do regard the racist and the niggerologist, metaphorically speaking, as first cousins. Here we may ask, What is a niggerologist?

From a cross-cultural conceptual framework, I mean to suggest that a niggerologist is a person who possesses a distorted image of the moral self by virtue of the desire to mirror the worth of oneself always through the narrow cultural lens of white Anglo-Saxon Protestantism. The sin of the niggerologist is the tendency to *privately* internalize, uncritically, the mannerisms, sentiments, and values of white folk, while *publicly* rebelling and railing against these inherent values. Like the prodigal son in the biblical story, the niggerologist is on a "trip" into a strange and far country. Metaphorically, it is a far country of hedonistic thrills, folly, and wastefulness, in which the niggerologist only discovers with dismay that when the laughter ceases and the money runs out—one's solitary soul finds itself face-to-face with the phenomenon of emptiness and dread, on a dead-end street.

In this scenario the niggerologist, unlike his first cousin the racist, is a de-centered self in a competitively fragmented society of conflicting narratives, where the only *center* that seems to matter revolves around power, privilege, and prejudice. In short, the authentic personhood of the niggerologist has been co-opted and de-centered not simply because of the tough times of black life in urban America but also because of the residual forces of white racism that gradually strip away the garment of human dignity from us all. For the niggerologist, like the racist bigot, there is a profound loss of self-esteem and morality. Nonetheless, to be a niggerologist also means the uncritical acceptance of another's definition of one's own worth and being. In the idiom of Afrocentric culture and moral tradition, for example, a noted black preacher, Bill Gillespie—who has served as pastor of Cote Brilliante Presbyterian Church, St. Louis, Missouri, for more than thirty-five years—warns us against the seductive nature of niggerology in terms of the ontology of ethnic relations in America today. In the rhythmic flow of proverbial "black talk," Gillespie emphatically asserts:

> Be what you is,
> and not what you ain't;
> because if you ain't what
> you is: you is
> what you ain't![14]

Ethically considered, I think that there are certain elements in the culture of gangsta rap music that not only serve to degrade our youth and disrespect the wisdom tradition of the elders but also prevent us all from being our true selves as children of God.

Furthermore, the basic contention of this writer is that while niggerism or niggerology may have its origins in the crucibles of slavery and European colonialism, it is neither a viable alternative to racism nor a justifiable reaction to the social situation of black suffering on the contemporary American scene. From a covenant-harambee frame of reference, it seems to me that the morally sensitive Christian of the black community has an obligation to tell the truth about the dangers of niggerology. Bonhoeffer reminds us, for instance, that "telling the truth means something different according to the particular situation in which one stands."[15]

In his widely read book *Ethics*, Dietrich Bonhoeffer provides the reader with further insights into what it means to tell the truth in terms of its contextual implications for people who use the language of "nigger" or "bitch." We must simply ask, What is meant by nigger? just as we ask, What is meant by "telling the truth"? Concerning the relationality and contextuality of truth-telling, Bonhoeffer writes:

> "Telling the truth," therefore, is not solely a matter of moral character; it is also a matter of correct appreciation of real situations and of serious reflection upon them. The more complex the actual situations of a man's life, the more responsible and the more difficult will be his task of "telling the truth"... Telling

---

[14]Enoch H. Oglesby, *Born in the Fire: Case Studies in Christian Ethics and Globalization* (New York: Pilgrim Press, 1990), pp. 116–119.

[15]Dietrich Bonhoeffer, *Ethics* (New York: Macmillan, 1955), p. 363.

the truth is, therefore, something which must be learnt. This will sound very shocking to anyone who thinks that it must all depend on moral character and that if this is blameless, the rest is child's play. But the simple fact is that the ethical cannot be detached from reality, and consequently continual progress in learning to appreciate reality is a necessary ingredient in ethical action.[16]

It seems to me that Bonhoeffer's principle of telling the truth is applicable to our current discussion of niggerism and racism, in the sense of their relationship to each other in a particular context. For example, they both offer a Draconian account of what is wrong with American culture. To be morally honest, if we say that racism is wrong for America, that racism is dangerous to your health and wellness, we must also say that niggerism is wrong for America; that it is also dangerous to one's health and the wellness of a nation. Both niggerism and racism are inflammatory. Both niggerism and racism dehumanize women and children. To be sure, real people of decency and conscience would not, for example, want to be called either a "racist" or a "nigger." Both are morally abhorrent. However, it is worth repeating that *real* people who live in the *real* world of white America cannot politically equate niggerism and racism as having the *same* power, except the power of humiliation. Furthering our ethical discussion, let us now look at five myths regarding the term *nigger.*

Five Myths about Niggerism

Ethically, it is only a glimpse into the obvious to suggest that people are not born into the world as "nigger" or "racist." I believe that people are not born with a natural inclination toward niggerism or racism; rather, these are acquired through certain religio-cultural habits and attitudes in our families, our schools, our churches, and our institutions of higher learning.

Contextually, the burden of the ethical demands that we "tell the truth" about the dangers of niggerism in our common life, as women and men of faith. But in light of the myths that need to be unmasked, the moral agent is obligated to come to terms with a *contextual* under-

---

[16]Ibid., pp. 364–365.

standing of truth—to paraphrase Dietrich Bonhoeffer. What then, are the dangers?

In the first place, there is the dangerous myth of stereotyping, implicit in human behavior on the part of parents, preachers, theologians, or secular persons. It takes the form of a simple attack on all "rappers" based on moral grounds. Conceptually, I think Bonhoeffer is essentially correct in suggesting that "telling the truth is not solely a matter of moral character." We cannot afford to assume, necessarily, that rappers per se are less moral than we are. For example, we have both good rappers and bad rappers. For within the culture of the rapper, the imperative of "telling the truth" is not contingent upon the presence or absence of moral character in the rapper: that would be tantamount to prejudgment and the subsequent misjudgment of one's true character.

In the second place, Christians and morally sensitive persons must be aware of the danger of self-righteousness. By this I mean the perfectionistic impulse in pretending that "we" have never engaged—by thought, word, or deed—in the nasty game of calling another human being "nigger." What is needed, I think, is the sort of courage that leads to confession and repentance. The Bible clearly teaches us that confession is good for the soul. As one honest rapper once remarked on the troublesome streets of St. Louis concerning the culture of rap music:

> Listen up, dude, this stuff
> done got out of hand…we
> need to 'fess up to our
> sin…of "nigger-this," "nigger-that,"
> what are we really passing onto these
> young dudes who look up to us
> as role models?[17]

---

[17]Jamal Cotham, unpublished interview. As a researcher on the cultural idiom of "black talk," I had the opportunity to interview a street rapper of the urban ethos of north St. Louis (i.e., predominantly the African American community), known as Brother Jamal. Who argued that the demonic forces of urban violence, drugs, family abuse, racism, and gangsta rap music had somehow made "niggas" of us all—regardless of social position, occupational status, or class stratum in the wider society. As a street rapper, Brother Jamal spoke of the need for positive role models across ethnic lines to counter the gradual trend toward the "niggeration" of American culture. "Young dudes gotta put the brakes on this business of always calling each other nigga," says Brother Jamal.

Undoubtedly, there is a note of truth that rings through these poignantly jagged words. For many, they simply remind us that we all sin when we choose to call another human being—for whatever reasons—"nigger." In the third place, there is the dangerous myth of an easy conscience which says that the word "nigger" really doesn't hurt anybody; that it is purely a sassy form of speech. Indeed, some go as far as to suggest that for us blacks, it is really a term of *endearment*, like a *fraternal rite of passage*, the true brothers-in-the-hood! To which I reply with a resounding NO!—pure and simple! The real acid test of this myth is, for instance, to be at a certain social gathering in serious conversation with one's friend from a different cultural background (e.g., a Caucasian or Latino friend), when suddenly the friend begins the conversation by saying: "Hey, what's up, nigger? I haven't seen you in a mighty long time!" Now, if you happen to be African American and this sort of thing occurs, please be prepared for a microcosm of World War III! Ethically, the bottom line is that such a scenario may inevitably give to the "outsider" mixed messages. In short, this is the reverse myth of a "double-standard." For example, how can the moral agent justify the use of the word "nigger" as a *black thing*? In a multicultural and multiracial society, is that the image or "thing" we want to personify as the normative basis for interracial friendship? Ethically, I don't think so!

In the fourth place, there is the dangerous myth of "turning the table" on the white racist oppressors, who—after all—created this offensive WORD and built a whole slave system and plantation culture around it. Psychologically, some misguided black intellectual may reason, "We're only taking a dirty name or word and cleaning it up, by giving it new content." But in my own mind, I can hear the words of Jesus quietly resounding deep in my soul: "You can't put new wine into old wine skins." The Bible warns us concerning this reality:

> No one sews a piece of unshrunk cloth on an old cloak, for the patch pulls away from the cloak…Neither is new wine put into old wineskins; otherwise, the skins burst, and the wine is spilled, and the skins are destroyed; but new wine is put into fresh wineskins, and so both are preserved. (Mt. 9:16–17)

In the fifth place, there is the myth of *verbal innocence,* and the failure to recognize that niggerism itself is a subtle form of violence and abuse against the human spirit. The ideology of niggerism contributes to what Carter G. Woodson calls the "mis-education of the Negro." Furthermore, the ideology of niggerism is morally wrong because it merely substitutes, from a historical perspective, the physical chains on one's legs for psychological chains on one's mind. In a multicultural and multiracial society, there is no place for either. The myth of verbal innocence also buys into the false claim that "sticks and stones may break my bones, but talk don't bother me." Well, the truth of the matter is that "stones" can break bones, but "words" can injure far more deeply by breaking the human spirit. Thus we are summoned by the force of conscience and by the living word of God to be morally vigilant against all forms of niggerism and racism. In a word, to be a follower of Jesus Christ means to be both an antiracist and antiniggerologist. Accordingly, we may define the latter as any person who becomes a *moral advocate against the use of the inflammatory term "nigger" by any ethnic group member—whether black or white—because of its negativity and slave origins in the Americas.* In short, the imposition of "niggerology" in whatever cultural form—either Eurocentrism or Afrocentrism—is ethically untenable and works against the common good of humanity.

Children in the Shadow, Children of the Dawn

Thus far in our discussion or interpretive analysis of the loathsome problems of racism and niggerism, we have suggested that they are closely related in terms of their adverse impact on the cultural and moral fabric of human community. We have also attempted to argue that the phenomenon of niggerism, as understood through the lens of historical studies and narrative accounts, apparently had its origins in the crucibles of chattel slavery and in the patterns of European colonialism in the early seventeenth century. As is so often the case with oppressed people and the human struggle for liberation, the first stages of creative protest must be against the *tendency of the victimized to turn on each other* in patterns of self-destruction and antisocial behavior.

In my judgment, the ideology of niggerism follows this peculiar pattern. In short, we have argued that niggerism as "first cousin" to racism is a form of misplaced aggression. In the cultural idiom of the black church experience, it follows the old individualistic philosophy of "crabs-in-the-bucket." Analytically, this brings us full circle, as it were, in our discussion of the dialectics of racism and niggerism as first cousins, because what is at stake inevitably is the future of our children and youth in human society. To put the matter sharply, given the demonic forces of racism and niggerism, will they be children in the shadow or children of the dawn?

Ethical reflection on the critical and varied problems in contemporary society can take many forms. Therefore, I wish to illustrate these socio-ethical issues by briefly looking at "black-on-black violence" in our society. Here it is my fundamental moral conviction that both racism and niggerism negatively feed into the phenomenon of so-called "black-on-black violence"—though not necessarily in the same way. On one level, it seems to me that the presence of violence today is critically tied in with the anatomy of poverty and the reality of racism in the context of American society. The dominant host culture sets the historical context in which the deadly game of black-on-black violence is acted out. Now on a narrative level, let us meet, for example, a St. Louis teenager by the name of Brian Easter, who is, metaphorically, one of the "children in the shadow, hoping to become a child of the dawn." Listen to the penetrating story of Brian Easter, a bright, energetic student from north St. Louis who wants to go to college one day. He complains to a friend:

> There's a lot of us dying out there over silly stuff. So I don't go out a lot. If you do go somewhere you have to watch your back.[18]

The North Side neighborhood where Brian lives is one of the city's most hostile environments. It is a place where the temptations of violence, gangs, and drugs are the garments that too many try on. It is a community teeming with the reality of parental ambivalence and racial polarization. It is a place where some of the most violent

---

[18]Brian Easter, "Native Sons: Inside the Lives of Young Black Men," in *Take Five Mazagine*, 6/2 (May/June 1993), p. 8. This article deals essentially with a socio–historical perspective on the contemporary problem of youth crime, especially the epidemic rate among young black men, in the city of St. Louis, Missouri. Here a cross-section of African American males talk candidly about their fears and hopes and what life is like as a member of an endangered species.

crimes are committed against innocent victims. It is a place where too many of our babies of color grow up too fast and die too young—being denied the opportunities for life, self-esteem, education and human wholeness. It has been said and some believe that the clue to the destiny of children of color can be seen in this comparative scenario regarding the life chances of the average ghetto black child in America:

He is twice as likely as a white baby to die in infancy.

He is more likely than a white to be malnourished and to need remedial education.

His life expectancy is about six years less than a white baby boy's. And if he dies in the first fifteen or so years of adulthood, the most likely cause will be homicide.

There is a 45 percent chance he will be the victim of violent crimes three or more times in his life.

He is less likely than a white to complete high school or college.

At today's rate, his family will earn $56 for every $100 earned by a white family.[19]

Undoubtedly, Brian Easter is painfully right in his observations that living in the "hood" or on the mean streets of St. Louis demands adherence to the rule of survival: "You have to watch your back." Like many other large urban centers in the nation, the plague of violence in St. Louis is tearing at the moral and social fabric of inner city black communities—especially among our youths. It is my contention that in a racist and increasingly niggerist society, the problem of violence is more greatly aggravated among black youths because of the long history of racial discrimination and economic exploitation in the American social system. Social critic Franz Fanon reminded us that an oppressed, victimized people often turn on each other rather than on the system which is oppressing them. Thus we pose the critical question slightly differently. Namely, in the case of Brian, will the gravity of life in the "hood" reflect a murky shadow or the breaking of the dawn for a new day?

In the final analysis, whether we as moral agents in church and society can adequately respond to this hurting dilemma regarding

---

[19]Patrick E. Gauen, "Uneven Odds: Dim Outlook Hinders Poor Blacks' Struggle," in *St. Louis Post-Dispatch* (Summer, 1993), p. 11.

the contextual reality of Brian Easter is, ultimately, not the main issue. The really hard ethical issue ever before us is this: Can we be honest with God and with each other about facing the demons of racism and niggerism, looking them dead in the eyes without blinking? Or must we as moral agents forever remain children in the shadow? On the one hand, given the irony and blood-soaked history of black people in the modern era, we must say that if racism persists as a permanent feature of American society—then I am afraid that it will remain frozen in the *shadow*. On the other hand, if niggerism persists in our society as "first cousin" and as a cultural form of alienation—then the voices of hope will be silenced. But if we face these moral dilemmas with courage and honesty—then the painful pregnancy of hope will give birth to tomorrow's children of the dawn. Such a metaphor of the dawn is poignantly expressed in S. Courtney Booker III's poem, "Tear of Hope":

> Today I cried
> However, my tears were filled with hope
> Hoping for a better tomorrow
> Hoping for a better life
>
> I see success around me
> Yet it's difficult to touch
> Uncanny in its elusiveness
> When will I grasp the brass ring
> When will I win the race
>
> My legs are tired
> But my heart is full of strength
> Tomorrow is the day
> I just know it is[20]

Stand Firm in the Lord against Racism and Niggerism

In retrospect, it seems to me that the persistent anguish of racism and niggerism in American life can, in fact, lay heavy upon the human spirit. Therefore, I suspect that some brief theological reflection upon these cultural anomalies is appropriate. From the perspective of our

---

[20]Cited in *Calendar of National Black Child Development Institute,* (Washington, D.C., 1995 Annual Conference) September.

previous discussion on ethical method, the language of covenant-harambee encourages the moral agent to stand firm in the Lord against all forms of racism and niggerism in our culture. The language of covenant-harambee invites the true followers of Jesus Christ to participate in the ethical intensification of all theological concepts in the perennial struggle for liberation and reconciliation. Obviously, racism and niggerism work against the ultimate goals of authentic freedom and unity in the body of Christ. But the true followers of Jesus Christ are compelled, by the liberating power of the Holy Spirit, to walk to the "beat of a different drummer" in confronting the demons of racism and niggerism in American culture.

For the Christian community of faith, the metaphor of "standing firm in the Lord" means assuming a covenant-harambee posture of "over againstness": over against the forces of death (racism and niggerism), and embracing the forces of life (grace and discipleship). Moreover, the ethical intensification of our theological concepts in the covenant-harambee model is precisely what the church of Jesus Christ needs, if we are to fully understand the grace of God and God's claim of discipleship upon our lives.

The challenge to "stand firm in the Lord" may remind us of the ethical stance implicit in Bonhoeffer's famous book *Cost of Discipleship* (a great work published in November 1937). The cutting edge of his ethico-theological thought is the distinction he makes between the interpretive categories of "cheap grace" and "costly grace." Bonhoeffer emphatically proclaimed:

> Cheap grace means the justification of sin without the justification of the sinner. Grace alone does everything, they say, and so everything can remain as it was before. "All for sin could not atone." The world goes on in the same old way, and we are still sinners....
>
> Cheap grace is the preaching of forgiveness without requiring repentance, baptism without church discipline, Communion without confession, absolution without personal confession. Cheap grace is grace without discipleship, grace without the cross, grace without Jesus Christ ....[21]

---

[21]Dietrich Bonhoeffer, *The Cost of Discipleship* (New York: Macmillan, 1963), pp. 46–47.

In a theologically brilliant contrast, Dietrich Bonhoeffer goes on to make the following distinction which has ethical implications for our current discussion:

> Costly grace is the treasure hidden in the field; for the sake of it a man will gladly go and sell all that he has. It is the pearl of great price to buy which the merchant will sell all his goods. It is the kingly rule of Christ, for whose sake a man will pluck out the eye which causes him to stumble, it is the call of Jesus Christ at which the disciple leaves his nets and follows him...
>
> Such grace is costly because it calls us to follow, and it is grace because it calls us to follow Jesus Christ.[22]

It seems to me that one of the ethical implications in our reflections on the phenomena of racism and niggerism is to simply suggest that without taking a firm stand against social evils in society, we commit the sin of "cheap grace." Put another way, we Christians simply participate—consciously or unconsciously—in maintaining the prevailing norms of the status quo. Undoubtedly, a second ethical implication which bears upon our life and witness against the demonic forces of racism and niggerism stems from the importance of naming the indispensability of "costly grace." Here the language of "costly grace" means the church is bound together in a covenant of radical love, disciplineship, and faith to "tell the truth" about the inherent dangers of racism and niggerism; and to warn both friend and foe that—without standing firm in the Lord— the followers of Christ may become permanent victims of "cheap grace."

In any event, the metaphor of "standing firm in the Lord" against the evil forces of racism and niggerism means recognizing the high price of "costly grace." It means a willingness to go the second mile for a homeless child or a confused adolescent who finds himself/herself caught up in the web of urban violence, hopelessness, and racial polarization. It means understanding the human self not as a passive spectator in somebody else's history but as a proactive agent in one's own ethnic history.

In short, standing firm in the Lord means a stubborn determination, as one made in the image of God (*Imago Dei*), to accept neither

---

[22]Ibid., pp. 46–47.

racism nor niggerism as the final word for the future in "minority-majority" relationships in the United States. Indeed, I think that this powerfully engaging metaphor, "standing firm in the Lord," may be the sort of eschatological symbol that can lead, for example, confused and troubled African American youths toward a better future, by taking seriously the ambiguity and promise of our collective struggle against both racism and niggerism.

4

A Vision beyond the
Mountain

*Humankind has not woven
the web of life. We are
but one thread within it.
Whatever we do to the web,
We do to ourselves. All things
are bound together. All
things connect.*

—Chief Seattle

Facing Hard Questions in Ministry

From an Afrocentric frame of reference, it is my deep moral conviction that there is no easy theological formula for critical reflection on the difficult question of racism in Christian ministry today. In pondering the whole matter a floodgate of hard questions seems to rush to the forefront of one's ethical consciousness. For example: What is ethnic diversity? What does diversity mean in the context of Christian ministry, especially for a people with a shared memory of suffering and hope? To make relevant Paul Lehmann's classical question of ethical discourse, the moral agent may logically ask: What am I, as a follower of Jesus and member of the Christian

95

community, to do about the mountain of racism? Can one be racist and Christian too? What is the faithful and loving thing to do when confronted—suddenly—with unanticipated bigoted attitudes among colleagues and friendly neighbors? What kind of ethical credo may contribute to a constructive understanding of "diversity" in the Christian moral life? Can one person, with God, really make a difference in reducing the high cost of racism in our church life and culture? Can the church of Jesus Christ, as a serving community of faith, really scratch where people itch?

These sorts of questions, I submit, are not easy to answer at the dawn of a new century, but they do swell inside morally sensitive persons attempting to "prime the pump" in search of a common ground for dialogue in struggling with the broader issue of ethnic diversity.

Rumblings and Ethnic Diversity: What Is All the Rumbling about and What Is Ethnicity?

People in "mainline" white middle class churches—small and large, throughout the heartland of America—realize that something is happening. They hear the echoes and see the rumblings; they often ponder from a distance the musings and groanings that give concrete expression to moral struggle on the part of those who live on the ragged edges of survival in Third World countries. The echoes and rumblings signal, in part, the emergence of a precarious vision, deeply imbedded in the hearts and souls of the poor and marginalized, that one day the world will be at peace, and the shouts of justice and freedom will replace death-dealing structures of tyranny and oppression. The echoes and rumblings signal in the trenches of an unjust world a desperate cry—from the bottom up— "let my people go!"

Although we are faced today in the global community with a growing mosaic of misery and death, the echoes and rumblings still signal the explosion of hope and faith that God will make right what a rebellious people have made wrong. The echoes and rumblings signal a stubborn faith in a freeing and unfailing God who is not finished with the frail and earthen vessel we call the church, the *ecclesia*, as she ponders and defines her mission and calling at the threshold of the twenty-first century. To a pilgrim people of faith, the echoes and rumblings signal a precarious vision of oneness and togetherness—captured in part by what many ethical theologians and leaders of the church refer to as the spirit of *harambee* (Swahili word for "unity"). Indeed, the echoes and rumblings signal a dream of human wholeness; they signal an understanding of Christian ministry inclusive of "God's rainbow kingdom," which has the capacity to generate human energy and to renew our family, church, and national life.

The perceptive poet Bill Strickland reminds us of the crucial importance of self-definition in understanding the social world. From an Afrocentric frame of reference, my own ethical sensibility and faith would lead me to contend that the world of ethnicity and Christianity is a socially constructed world, in the sense that all human reality is socially constructed reality. "The first right of a people who want to be free is the right to define their own reality,"[1] says Strickland. Therefore, we ponder in our deep moments of faith the complex and thorny issue of ethnic diversity. Conceptually speaking, we may use the term "ethnicity," in the context of our struggle against racism, to refer to the *cohesive presence, moral values, beliefs, and customs of certain ethnic groups seeking to respect and live in harmony with one another in human community.*

Etymologically, the notion of "ethnicity" stems from the Greek word *ethnos,* which literally means "people" or "nation"—and a sense

---

[1]Cited in *Report on the Third Annual Black Church Studies Fall Convocation* (St. Louis: Eden Seminary Office of Continuing Education, October, 1989), p. 1ff. The theme for the convocation was "Seeking God's Righteousness: The Church Confronts Racism and Oppression." Here a group of more than 200 African American Christians, clergy, seminarians, and international students attended the two-day conference. In terms of church participation and religious pluralism, the variables in denominational representation included: Baptist, Methodist, Presbyterian, Lutheran, U.C.C., Catholic, Seventh-Day Adventist, Church of God in Christ, Disciples of Christ, and Muslim. Dr. Samuel Hylton, the keynote conference speaker, strongly emphasized a biblically grounded basis for global awareness and ethnicity as people of goodwill confront the demons of racism and oppression in the world. Accordingly, he suggested three pivotal points: "(a) Our Lord Jesus began his own ministry by quoting from the book of Isaiah, chapter 61. Jesus' ministry was to liberate and to set people free from the spiritual, physical, social and economic confinements that inhibit the abundant life. (cf. Lk. 4:18); (b) Christian faith is a call to social action and justice; this is why we (Christians) are here; and; (c) Justice is a process of sorting out what rightfully belongs to other people and then giving it back to them." (pp. 2–5).

of loyalty to certain prevailing values, both subjective and objective. At the subjective level, there is present among all ethnic groups certain sentiments and emotional ties between members which are nurtured and sustained by their shared heritage and experience.[2] At the objective level, there is the recognition and growing need for political coalitions, moral agency, and cooperative action in seeking the common good—especially the need for economic empowerment and full human liberation on behalf of African Americans, Hispanics, Asians and other minorities. Thus the struggle to understand and to do ministry in a multicultural and multiracial playground of the world is the life and faith of the church and presents a real challenge for the church in our time. It means an understanding of the reality of "ethnic diversity" as a gift to be shared rather than a menacing threat to what C. Eric Lincoln calls the "host culture" of America.[3] Accordingly, the reality of ethnic diversity is a way of affirming and respecting the moral and religious beliefs and customs of another social group. Normatively considered, the real imperative is the need for a sense of "we-ness" or cohesion in "ethnic diversity," which rules out the sinful vices of social exclusiveness and racial hostility.

Moreover, I think that those who affirm the importance of inclusivity and the principle of ethnic diversity are obligated to resist in the name of Jesus Christ all blatant forms of ethnocentricism. By definition, ethnocentrism, in contrast to ethnic diversity, denotes the tendency of most people—especially religious bigots—to use their own culture and way of life as the sole standard for judging others; such persons also tend to see their own race or culture as inherently superior to all others. Hence, *ethnocentrism* is a very

---

[2]Deepak K. Behera, *Ethnicity and Christianity* (Kashmere Gate, Delhi: Indian Society for Promoting Christian Knowledge, 1989), p. 32ff. The reader may also note that emerging terms such as "multiculturalism," "transculturalism," or "interculturalism" are part and parcel of the new language of globalization ethics and missiology as the church struggles with questions of identity and purpose in the world at the threshold of the twenty-first century. For example, Edwina Hunter defines interculturalism as a process of deep sharing and a willingness to be vulnerable to the gifts and values of others.

[3]Cited in C. Eric Lincoln's unpublished address "Black Church Experience and Ethnicity in America" (St. Louis: St. Paul AME Church, Feb., 1992).

pejorative term which goes beyond a mere preference for and pride in one's own cultural heritage to the point of "put-down" or the subordination of another person or an entire group of people based on skin color, language, and psychosocial differences. In short, what I am trying to suggest is the importance of an analytic distinction between *ethnocentrism* and the positive phenomenon of ethnic diversity.

Ethnicity and Theology

The liberation theologian J. Deotis Roberts, in his book *A Black Political Theology*, draws a significant link between ethnicity and theology, given the long history of black suffering in America.[4] From a historical perspective, for example, our feelings about peoplehood and ethnic diversity have been more dynamic than static in depicting the theological problem of race relations today. Roberts asserts:

> The theology of race relations has centered around the fatherhood of God and the brotherhood of man. God and society were seen as relating to individuals rather than to races and groups. Reform would result in from individual regeneration apart from membership in self-conscious racial or cultural groups. But now we are beginning to realize that racial and cultural differences are important factors for understanding and appreciating the complexity and variety of the human family.[5]

Theologically, it is enormously important to underscore the spiritual and cultural link between African Americans and black Africans. Though scarred and distorted by centuries of oppression and colonialistic exploitation, black people living in America do, in fact, share a sense of common ancestry with black Africans, especially West Africans.[6] "There is continuity as well as discontinuity between the African past of black Americans," says Roberts, "and their present situation."[7] He further argues (and I think rightly so) that

---

[4]J. Deotis Roberts, *A Black Political Theology* (Philadelphia: Westminster Press, 1974), p. 49.
[5]Ibid.
[6]Ibid., p. 50.
[7]Ibid.

"Black American culture is synthetic."[8] In seeking to grasp the complex pattern of continuity vis-à-vis discontinuity in the African American religio-cultural heritage, there is a cryptic proverb which reads: "the blood that unites us is thicker than the water that divides us." Here the human cry is for a broader sociohistorical perspective which engages the world and challenges the so-called Christian churches of North America to be open to the universal yearnings for dignity, justice, and genuine freedom on the part of the poor and oppressed.

Perhaps one of the important recent works to address this complexity, the perennial problem of ethnicity, theology, and racism, on a broader scale is the provocative book *Jesus in Global Contexts* by Priscilla Pope-Levison and John R. Levison. These authors strongly argue that one of the things Latin American people, in both church and society, share with people of color in North American culture is a profound sense of economic, social, and political dependency. Thus, liberation theologians cite the factor of dependency as a critical restraint on the church which prevents full participation in societal transformation. For example, these authors also point out that the perennial economic and racist exploitation of the poor has led, in part, to a two-tiered process of dependency in Latin American culture. Accordingly, Priscilla Pope-Levison and John Levison wrote the following:

> The first tier consists of Latin America's dependency on foreign countries and foreign investments. This external dependency has been forged since colonization when its human and economic resources were ravaged by other countries. Many countries have been part to Latin America's dependency, including Spain, Portugal, Great Britain, the Soviet Union, and the United States of America. External dependency on other countries, the first tier, has created an internal dependency within the region, which constitutes the second tier. In this second tier, the poor majority are dependent on the ruling class, a slim minority who control the social, economic, and political spheres of life.[9]

---

[8] Ibid., pp. 49–54.
[9] Priscilla Pope-Levison and John R. Levison, *Jesus in Global Contexts* (Louisville: Westminster/John Knox Press, 1992), p. 26.

We may observe that there are both internal and external patterns of dependency rooted in the seductive power of the ruling class; but these complex socioeconomic patterns are closely linked with foreign powers—largely multinational corporations in both the United States and Europe. The upshot of this observation is as simple as it is awesome: the reality of racism is not only multidimensional but also transcontinental. In a word, the demonic force of racism significantly affects economic, social, and political developments around the world.

Ethnicity as Contextual Narrative

According to Stanley Hauerwas in his book *A Community of Character*, we as morally sensitive Christians are all influenced by the power of cultural narratives—whether they be negative or positive. Through our critical study of biblical theology and Christian ethics, for instance, we have come to see that the church, the *ecclesia*, is not only an assembly of God's people, the body of Christ, but also a "story-formed community."[10] Thus, the difficult issues of faith and life do not take place in a vacuum but within the tensions and cultural polarities of this present social order—i.e., the tensions between forces of justice and injustice, between immoral power and powerless morality, between the haves and the have-nots, between black and white, between men and women, between the conflicting impulses of "holding on and letting go," and, implicit in the dialectical rhythms, the tensions between experience and expectation.

In a story-shaped world of pain and promise, it seems to me that we have learned at least three things about the nature of Christian social ethics and its implications for ethnic relations in contemporary society. Here we must remember that a) "every social ethic involves a narrative, whether it is concerned with the formulation of basic principles of social organization and/or concrete policy alternatives; b) the social significance of the Gospel requires the recognition of the narrative structure of Christian convictions for the life of the church; and c) the ability to provide an adequate account of our existence is the primary test of the truthfulness of a social

---

[10]Stanley Hauerwas, *A Community of Character: Toward a Constructive Christian Social Ethic* (Notre Dame: University of Notre Dame Press, 1981), pp. 9–19.

ethic."[11] Given the interrelated character of Christian theology and social ethics, we may say "so far, so good." Indeed, Hauerwas is correct, I think, in suggesting that these are some of the central normative presuppositions which enable us to see that the church is a community formed by a "truthful narrative" whose center is Jesus Christ. Theologically, this is the redemptive story of grace and freedom, because of a man called "Jesus of Nazareth."

But we also have—comparatively and culturally—the demonic story of racial prejudice in the United States. To put the matter succinctly, nearly every morally honest person knows that there is a difference between Christian ethics and the ethics of Christians, when it comes to the painful issue, existentially, of racism. Therefore, I wish to share a *narrative snapshot* from the chronicles of my own experience as a black professor on the faculty of Eden Theological Seminary. This narrative is not fictional, but true; and it is still, surprisingly, painful for me to share after all these years. But existentially, I know that I dare not remain *privatistic* in my pain, and must lay bare my soul, though the risk of vulnerability is ever-present in the community—but even more important, I lay bare my soul amid the healing waters of God's grace.

To paraphrase, in part, the narrative ethics of Stanley Hauerwas, allow me "to provide an adequate account of my existence," here in the community of Eden Seminary during my first year on the faculty back in 1978. The particular racial incident occurred over the Labor Day weekend at a cookout at the home of one of my colleagues in Webster Groves, Missouri. As was our faculty custom, we would usually gather voluntarily as friends and families to, as it were, "break bread together" and to psychologically bone up for the exciting challenges, academic burdens, and blessings of a new entering class into the life of our "beloved Eden," the school and intellectual nursery of two of Eden's most famous sons: H. Richard and Reinhold Niebuhr. With theological readiness and eagerness over the size of the new class of seminarians, a Promethean spirit of excitement filled the campus air, as if Ozzie Smith of the St. Louis Cardinals just came up to bat and knocked a home run in the World Series. Accordingly, the precipitating issue was over the *number* of the minority students entering Eden and not the "size" of the

---

[11]Ibid., pp 9–10.

class as a whole.You see, the numbers of blacks were up by a few from the previous year. Naturally, my wife and I were excited about this most significant sign of progress, of which I remarked: "You know, it's a wonderful thing that we have more black students…" With a serious look on his face, a white, male colleague sharply replied: "Enoch, we don't want too many blacks here…because 'they' will lower our academic standards!"

In shock and speechless, I looked at my wife and my wife looked at me, and then the conversation rapidly moved on to a more "pleasant" topic of the evening. Quietly angered and subdued, I felt speechless, voiceless, and stunned over the verbal impact of such a revelatory attitude expressed by a colleague I held in high esteem. With the utterance of that split second, all that I knew or held in sacred trust about the intellectual and cultural achievements of black people in America became—deep in my soul—momentarily neutralized. In short, I became silenced by this revelatory attitude in our "garden of Eden." Looking back upon that watershed experience as the first black man called to serve full-time on the faculty in the history of the institution, I was fairly warned by Dr. Allen O. Miller, a senior colleague and friend, who said to me: "Brother Enoch, this place may be the idyllic garden of Eden…but watch out for the snakes!" Be that as it may, my brain was still apparently silenced by the impact of this racial offense and indignity suffered by my wife and me.

From a conceptual frame of reference, Darryl Trimiew, in his book *Voices of the Silenced: The Responsible Self in a Marginalized Community*, describes for me the pain of that moment, at a friendly cookout on the "corner" of the Eden campus, by distinguishing between two interpretive categories of human ethical discourse.[12] The first distinction is to see the moral agent as essentially *homo dialogicus*, that is to say "dialogical humanity";[13] and the second distinction is to see the moral agent as *homo dialogicus marginalis*, which refers to a view of the moral agent as "marginalized dialogical humanity."[14] To be sure, this particular racial incident left no doubt in *our* minds as to the camp in which we belonged. Well, after a few fleeting moments

---

[12]Darryl M. Trimiew, *Voices of the Silenced: The Responsible Self in a Marginalized Community* (Cleveland: Pilgrim Press, 1993), p. xvii.

[13]Ibid., p. xvii.

[14]Ibid., pp. xvii–xix.

had passed, my wife and I soon made—as gracefully as possible—our exit for home. But this chilling incident upset us greatly, and left an indelible mark of Midwestern "Christian realism" upon our social consciousness as newcomers in the community. Ironically, our home on the "Eden faculty corner" (119 Bompart)—as I affectionately refer to it—is the same home, according to Evangelical oral tradition, that H. Richard Niebuhr had built and lived in while serving on the Eden faculty during the mid-1920s. Be that as it may, I suspect that the white-capped mountain of racism is alive and well in many educational vineyards of Midwestern culture—as would be the case for the nation at large. Ultimately, I suspect that our story is no more than an invisible microcosm that fills in the cracks in the foundation of a largely Eurocentric culture deeply burdened by the scourge of racism. In retrospect, however, I can truly say that the friendly cookout among "good people" and neighbors on the Eden faculty corner—over the Labor Day Weekend in 1978—is an occasion that will long be remembered by my wife and me. Ethically considered, I think that it would be well for us to ponder the words of Claude M. Steele, who once remarked concerning the problem of racism in America:

> Terms like "prejudice" and "racism" often miss the full scope of racial devaluation in our society, implying as they do that racial devaluation comes primarily from the strongly prejudiced, not from "good people." (In *Black Pearls* dated March 20)

Harambee Credo for the Church

From an Afrocentric frame of reference, it is important, I believe, to affirm—in our reflections upon the problem of racism in the wider Christian community of faith—who we are and whose we are. Theologically, many confess: "We are the people of God." But who are we? Socio-ethically it is obvious that within the context of American society we are a culturally complex and religiously diverse people. Similar to other social groups on the contemporary American scene, we also share in a credo of common experience in which many confess: "We are ordinary people who...go to work each day, who pay our taxes...who seek to live in decent and safe neighborhoods…who want to educate our children in a healthy and violence-free society…who fear God, and show kindness toward other persons not like us…" So far so good! This litany of normative confessions implies *harambee*. Whatever else we may say about the spirit of harambee for the church today, I believe it means the affirmation of the *ordinariness, concreteness,* and *interdependent* character of all human life as a people of faith under God.

Moreover, it is my fundamental suspicion that the answer to the culturally-laced question "Who are we?" is really rooted in the deeper theological question "*Whose* are we?" Here I mean to suggest, from an Afrocentric frame of reference, the positive value of a harambee-oriented credo for the church in our time. For example, the notion of credo, in the life and faith of the church, echoes the Latin words *cor* and *do,* meaning "to give one's heart to." As a person of faith, the Christian is called, therefore, to give one's heart and ultimate loyalty to Jesus, the Compassionate Liberator. Hence, the notion of credo refers to one's particular anchor of value and loyalty. It seems to me that the theological question "*Whose* are we?" can be answered in at least three ways in our reflections on a viable ethical credo, reflective of the spirit of harambee for the doing of Christian ministry in the world.

First, we believe in the *shout of love.* We confess that we are a community of disciples bound to Jesus Christ through our baptism and bound in genuine love and obedience to the work of ministry in the world. The virtue of love informs our understanding of who God is. In a theological sense, the virtue of love is neither passive-aggressive nor emotive-sentimental. Rather, genuine love is courageous goodwill in the interest of a revolutionary freedom initiated by God in the person of Jesus Christ. It invites us to participate in the dance of God and in the *shout of freedom!* Hence, we confess through the ethical credo that Jesus Christ is Liberator. "For freedom Christ has set us free. Stand firm, therefore, and do not submit again to a yoke of slavery" (Gal. 5:1).

Secondly, we believe in the *shout of faith.* The spirit of *harambee credo* for the church in our time must affirm—or so it seems to me—that we are all brothers and sisters in *faith.* Historically, the theological echoes of the great Reformers Luther and Calvin remind us that we are ultimately justified not by the ethic of "works righteousness," but by faith as active goodwill. We are justified by faith in the God of the Bible, who comes to us in the particularity of our own pain and suffering and offers to us hope and liberation from all forms of human oppression. Such a "faith," we confess, is never easy for the whole church to embrace, because it often demands relinquishing power and letting go of the loathsome, dominated values of possessive individualism, classism, sexism, and racism. To be sure, I believe that a viable ethical credo for the church in our time must find the strength and courage—by the grace of God—to resist these and other demonic "isms" which so easily beset us as human beings living in the modern world.

Thirdly, we believe that the spirit of harambee demands from us all a prophetic *shout of justice*. Here it seems to me that justice is the key imperative of a viable ethical credo in dealing with the plight of the poor and oppressed in the global community. Justice means giving to each child his or her due. For the church universal, the shout of justice can never be separated from the shout of love. For example, the actual work of harambee in the life and faith of the church does not emphasize "traditional charity" in the form of hand outs to the poor; but rather, it emphasizes equal justice in the interest of economic, political, and social change in the global community. The persistent *shout of justice*, as expressed by the biblical prophets of ancient Israel, means doing something with the poor rather than for the poor and marginalized ones in our midst. (Isa. 16–17; Amos 5:12; Isa. 3:14–15).

The liberal view of the church today seems to miss the boat precisely on this point, because of the tendency by many liberal Christians to equate charitable handouts with the presence of justice. The persistent *shout of justice* on the part of the disinherited demands from the church in our global community more than just a "handout," but a "hand": a *hand* that empowers the poor and the hurting ones. An old adage in the African American community puts it well: "Give a man a fish, you feed him for a day; teach a man how to fish, you feed him for a lifetime." The persistent *shout of justice*, then, empowers the powerless in the interest of their own dignity and the dignity of us all. Thus the *shouts* of *justice, faith, freedom,* and *love* belong together if we are to have a global vision beyond the slippery mountain of racism.

A Vision beyond the Mountain

It seems to me that a vision beyond the mountain, in the context of the global community, demands that we believe in a God of justice and love. Therefore, God is Justice-Love.[15] The prophets of old reminded us of both God's steadfast love and justice and warned the church of false worship: "Take away from me the noise of your songs...But let justice roll down like waters..." (Amos 5:23–24).

From an Afrocentric perspective, it seems to me that the church today is in trouble, not only because it lacks a coherent global vision beyond the mountain of racism, but also because of its preoccupation with maintenance over mission and respectability over credibility—in her feeble attempt to respond to the needs and cries of the hurting ones in our world. For example, the real gravity of this current ecclesial dilemma is cogently expressed by Frederick Herzog in his book *Justice Church.* He writes:

> Many of our churches still create an atmosphere of respectability. But they are living on borrowed capital, the memory of saintly souls, the spiritual aura still reflected in the religion sections of our newspapers, and the awe the label "Reverend" still exudes. So for awhile I concluded that what we are up against is a moral issue: *respectability on Sunday, credibility gaps on Monday—in the real world.*[16]

As much as we may stretch our souls to be seriously engaged in the practice of ministry today, the *elán vitale* of a harambee credo would insist that we close the credibility. Put in the Afrocentric idiom of the black church experience, the Christian faith of future generations will insist that our "God-talk" be consistent with our "God-walk," on matters of race and religion. And if by chance we have no ethical inclination to walk the God-walk, we ought to be careful about how we talk the God-talk! You see, somebody may

---

[15]Frederick Herzog, *Justice Church: The New Function of the Church in North American Christianity* (Maryknoll: Orbis Books, 1980), p. 81ff.

[16]Ibid., p. 8ff.

accuse—with justification—the "saints" of God with the sin of hypocrisy. In any event, I believe that the actual *work* of harambee in the church today demands coherence between God-talk and God-walk, between creeds and deeds, and between the beliefs we confess and the social values by which we live, if the wider society dares to overcome the mountain of racism. I wish to conclude, therefore, our reflections in this chapter regarding the need for a vision beyond the mountain.

Analytically, the following chart or typology seeks to relate and contrast an Afrocentric perspective vis-à-vis a Eurocentric perspective in regard to a vision beyond the mountain of racism. Such a vision demands "moral agency" as we ponder afresh the challenges and possibilities of doing Christian ministry in the twenty-first century. Here we shall briefly sketch or try to illuminate orientational aspects of moral agency as well as the interactive tensions implicit in our conceptual framework. Summarily, the chart visually includes:

Moral Agency and Racism: A Vision beyond the Mountain
Orientational Aspects

Eurocentric Form	*Afrocentric Form*
Moral agency learning *about* experiences of the oppressed	Moral agency learning through solidarity with the oppressed
Justice as human worth based on merit, or what you do	Justice as human worth based on equal regard, on who you are
If I'm not for myself who will be for me; I think, therefore, I exist	I am because we are; and because we are, therefore, I am
Ethical duality rooted in "Socratic-Cartesian view"	Ethical totality rooted in "kinship or covenant-harambee view" of the world
White church as Preserver of culture in a racist society	Black church as Transformer of culture in a racist society
Liturgy as ritualistic confession of faith—largely without reference to racism	Liturgy as spontaneous celebration of faith—largely as a bridge over the troubled waters of racism
Mission as Maintenance of moral tradition in the *oikumene*	Mission as Engagement in moral action for the sake of the *oikumene*
Racism as immoral power from the *top-down* (often unconscious by its perpetrators)	Racism as immoral power, challenged from the *bottom-up* (always consciously felt by its victims)
Racism as Prejudice plus power, giving whites privilege	Racism as Mountainous-humiliation plus *power-over*, giving people of color pain
Racism as system of institutional controls and justification for "Continuing business as usual", Racism as *sin of shame* without restitution or historic correction	Racism as an "idolatrous faith system" that must be dismantled for the wellness of the whole society
Racism as primarily a "white problem"	Racism as prophetic challenge to climb the slippery mountain

On one side of the chart or typology is designated certain essential elements as expressive of the "Eurocentric form" in the Christian moral life. The opposite side of the chart indicates an alternative reading of the Christian moral life by describing certain essential elements that symbolize an Afrocentric form or worldview. Analytically the two columns represents a contrast between the elemental perspectives of the "Eurocentric form" and the "Afrocentric form" in the struggle to better understand the complexities of Christian ministry and cultural diversity in a racist society. These "subjects" are not mutually exclusive in the being and doing of one's life orientation, but simply reflect *difference*. For example, in the covenant-harambee model of ethical discourse, the reality of *difference* does not automatically signal "deficiency" any more than the reality of a "Eurocentric form" necessarily signals "sufficiency." Logically and summarily, we are compelled to raise the following critical question, namely: What, then, is the vision beyond the mountain?

First, at the practical level in human community, the vision is nothing less than a bold Christian commitment to "moral agency" itself. Many of us who have engaged in the collective struggle for racial justice, equality, and freedom for decades in the United States *know*, deep in our souls, nothing comes without the ethical burden of commitment. Indeed, practical moral reasoning demands that we, as a pilgrim people of God, make hard moral choices about the perennial evils of racism in our culture. One can put the matter succinctly: either you are part of the *problem* or the *solution* to racism. Here moral agency clearly means a bold commitment to be part of the "solution." Moreover, I wish to suggest that the covenant-harambee model of ethical discourse sees moral agency as an instrument by which the individual seeks to overcome the treacherous mountain of racism in America. Also, the term "moral agency" in the context of the black religious experience means the capacity to actively engage in the moral struggle for liberation against the demonic forces of racism and all other "isms" that make us less than what God intended in the fragile web of human creation.

For example, moral agency is a way of being in the world which engages the individual in the critical process of discerning, naming, choosing, and acting for the sake of the "common good" (i.e., the vision of justice and community); and against the "common evil" (i.e., the burden of racism and oppression). The chart itself indicates a dynamic pattern of interaction. Ethically, it seems to me that the moral agent has an obligation to similarly "name" or tag the face of racism. Hence, we have argued, metaphorically, throughout the discussion that racism is *a treacherous mountain.*

Second, a vision beyond the mountain is one that affirms the value of persons-in-community. Each person is a child of God, possessing equal worth. The worth of persons cannot be determined by what we do, by mere achievements, or by a sociological variable used to measure one's sense of belonging to a particular ethnic group. Blind loyalty to any "color," in the defense of "ethnic purity" of any *type,* is no virtue. The worth of persons can neither be reduced to a sort of "thingified reality"—which is alienated from human community—nor can it be embodied in the Promethean relativism of *laissez faire* economics, which says: "The individual alone is the supreme measure of all things." To be sure, the worth of persons is not derived from a notion of selective membership in the *in-race* as being "superior" and, by contrast, the presence of one's membership in the *out-race* as being "inferior." It is important to observe that for people of color, the presence of racist ideology down through the centuries of social life in America has perpetuated this false dichotomy as a way to keep African Americans, Latinos, Asians, Native Americans, and others in "their place."

Despite significant progress, the marvelous achievements of the civil rights movement of the mid-'60s in dismantling the evils of *de jure* segregation in public life, we still must confess the lethal sin of racism, as the *conditio sine qua non* for the maintenance of a largely white male hierarchy in the American sociocultural system. In human community, the reality of moral agency demands that we confess racism as a destructive force which undermines the Christian virtues of love, righteousness, faith, long-suffering, joy, and the hope for racial harmony among ethnic peoples in this country. In human community, we confess that moral agency demands that racism should have no place in the public life, daily practices, and institutional policies of our social, economic, political, and religious institutions as a nation.

Third, a vision beyond the mountain of racism is an invitation to rethink and dialogue afresh concerning the purpose and mission of the church in a multicultural and multiracial society. Accordingly, the bold vision of the church as *human community* as articulated, in part, by H. Richard Niebuhr provides us with a functional perspective on the ecclesial—in discerning the complex sociocultural forces of ethnicity and faith in America today. In his classic volume *The Purpose of the Church and Its Ministry,* this noted theologian reminds us that the fundamental purpose of the Christian community is the "increase of the love of God and neighbor,"[17] as imaged in the radical teachings of the gospel of Jesus Christ. The church that is created by the suffering love of God, as revealed in Jesus Christ, is the one which acknowledges the norm of justice as a critical paradigm concerning matters of ethnicity and theological diversity. This means that agapeistic love is not sentimental goodwill in an abstract sense, but rather it is the presence of the reign of the "one God above many" as a new paradigm for human relatedness, especially in a society grappling with the evils of racism.

In the Evangelical and theologically liberal tradition of H. Richard Niebuhr, the morally honest Christian is challenged to affirm that the "increase of love of God and neighbor" must—necessarily—mean the love of justice as a theological norm, possessing the power to shape our vision of the *inclusive* community as a people of faith. Therefore, a viable vision is one that is open to the critical gifts and abilities of African Americans, Hispanics, Latinos, Asian Americans, Native Americans, and other people of color. Finally, a viable vision beyond the mountain of racism in our time must affirm the *love of justice* as imaged in the gospel of Jesus Christ. Therefore, such an image not only shapes and *forms* community, but through the power of the Holy Spirit can *transform* oppressive structures and racist attitudes of the wider society. The love of justice is the cost of true discipleship in our time. Jesus emphatically declared: "Seek first the kingdom of God and God's justice and all these things shall be added to you" (Mt. 6:33). To be sure the *raison d'etre* of our life together in human society is nothing less than the *love of justice* and the *justice of love.*

---

[17]H. Richard Niebuhr, *The Purpose of the Church and Its Ministry* (New York: Harper & Row, 1956) pp. 27–43.

What, then, must Euro American Christians be willing to confess? Well, I cannot say for sure. I am not a Euro-American. But I suspect that a minimum step up the slippery mountain of racism should include an acknowledgment, *ipso facto*, that racism has deeply impaired our vision of the inclusive community in the life of local white congregations. As one element of the human rainbow, comparatively speaking, what must African American Christians be willing to confess? Again, because I am black and proud of it, I do not presume to speak for some generic African American community; I can speak only for myself as a child of God. Nonetheless, I suspect that a minimum step up the treacherous mountain of racism in America demands letting go of a "slave mentality," a robust move to break psychologically the seductive chains of niggerism, uncritical bourgeois individualism, and the smothering virus of "crabs-in-a-bucketism" that siphons off our moral strength and spiritual solidarity—largely for the tasteless breadcrumbs of self-gain.

Here it seems to me that faithfulness to a wider vision, necessarily, must demand from us all not heroic strokes based on a distant utopian dream for a better society in the "sweet-bye-and-bye"— but rather a stubborn, unrelenting persistence in a multitude of small gestures loyal to the God-force of love and justice inside all of us. Ultimately, the love of justice—sufficiently stubborn to overcome the mountain of racism—demands nothing less; and faithfulness to the gospel of Jesus Christ demands nothing more. It is a sobering thought that the love of justice brings the Christian community face-to-face with the liberating power of the One God *above* the mountain who cracks open the frozen rocks of ethnic division and hatred in our troubled world. The One God above the mountain challenges the Christian community to live by the power of the spirit, which gives us the capacity to love the unlovable and to overcome the scourge of ethnic and class division in our time. If it is not asking too much of America on this perennial question of racism: *GIVE US THIS MOUNTAIN!*

Although we are fragmented beings wounded by the arrow of racism, the good news of the gospel of Jesus Christ is this: the moral insight that the contradictions of life are never final; that human life is a single statement; that there is no aspect of human experience—however marred by the demons of racial prejudice and bigotry—beyond the redeeming love of God in Jesus Christ. For the One God *above* the mountain is restless and free, nudging and inviting the whole church of Jesus Christ to continue its ministries of suffering love and reconciliation, and to journey toward racial harmony in search of the answer that is blowing in the wind. In the tattered and tested words of an old Negro spiritual, "Be Still, My Soul," for I can see, darkly, beyond the mountain a new vision of humanity. "Be Still, My Soul" for I can hear the faint voice of a new drummer which is beyond me and within me. "Be Still My Soul," for the One God *above* the mountain—has overcome the mountain.

A Selected Cultural Glossary

African experience—Refers to narrative accounts and influences during the period of the Patriarchs in relation to certain Old Testament personalities in the Bible such as Abraham, father of the Hebrews; Jacob, father of the Israelites; and Joseph, father of the two most important northern tribes of Israel, according to Copher. "Relative to Abraham it is recounted that because of famine in the land of Canaan he and his entourage...migrated to Egypt...It is further recounted that in Egypt, Abraham obtained an Egyptian maid, Hagar, by whom he sired his first-born son, Ishmael. For Ishmael, his mother obtained an Egyptian wife. In turn, Ishmael became the father of several progeny among whom was Kedar, the exceedingly black one, who became ancestor of several tribes in Asia," says Copher. In any event, the word "Egypt" occurs seventy-nine times in accounts involving the Hebrew Patriarchs and Joseph (See Copher's *Black Biblical Studies*, pp. 136–140).

Afro-acculturation—The social process by which African Americans as a group became organically linked to a new value system, social climate, or ethos based on one's own religious convictions and moral claims as individuals in human society. It is also a social process of conditioning characterized by conciliation, mutuality, and respect for cultural differences among all people in the world.

Afrocentricity—A philosophical system of inquiry that gives moral agency and subject-reality to people of African descent; it is the belief in the centrality of Africans as a *liberating* and *humanizing* force in postmodern history. Molefikete Asante, a renowned Afrocentrist in North America, has spoken in regard to the concept of Afrocentricity as "a transforming agent in which all things that were old become new and a transformation of attitudes, beliefs, values, and behavior results." (See Asante's book *Afrocentricity*, Trenton, N.J.: Africa World Press, Inc., 1991, pp. 1-2).

Afrophobia—Fear of people of African descent.

Amoral—A form of behavior by the moral agent that reflects

115

disregard for traditional categories of right and wrong, good and evil; broadly considered, a person who is wholly lacking in a sense of moral responsibility. Thus "racist behavior" cannot be dismissed as *amoral*, but "immoral," since most perpetrators of racism generally are aware of their behavior or conduct.

Anglophobia—Fear of people of European descent.

Antiniggerologist—An advocate against the use of the term "nigger" by any ethnic group members—whether black or white—because of its negativity and slave origin in the Americas.

Assimilation—The complex process by which different cultures, families, ethnic groups, or individuals representing divergent cultures are merged into another culture or a homogeneous unit. In North American society there is the dominant myth of the so-called "melting pot," but for people of African descent, ironically, the pot has lost its melting capability.

Bad faith—An existentialist term that conveys multiple meanings. For example, in black-white relations it may imply distrust of whites by blacks rooted in certain cultural sentiments of historical patterns of discrimination. For others, it may signal one who deals in falsehood or deception for self-gain.

Bad nigger—An "in-group" term that some African Americans use to describe blacks who are courageous, talented, flamboyant in style or dress; defiant of conventional Eurocentric values and beliefs; intellectually iconoclastic in human spirit.

Black thang—A reference to any ebonic speech pattern or social practice, custom, or cultural attitude arising from the African American experience.

Black theology—A branch of modern theology in North American culture which emphasizes that Christian theology is essentially a theology of liberation from white oppression, and from all forms of injustice and exploitation. This theological orientation tends to see Jesus Christ not only as norm for the moral life, but ultimately as Liberator and Reconciler of all humankind.

Black political theology—A form of theological discourse shaped in part by the social and cultural movements of the mid-sixties and seventies—with an emphasis on political liberation and economic empowerment of blacks and other ethnic groups, who have been traditionally locked out of full participation in the American democratic system.

British imperialism—The historical practice or "national policy" implicit in European culture and values that led, apparently, to the spirit of expansionism and the forcible annexation of adjoining territories or by the coercive strategy of gaining possession of alien lands and the subjugation of peoples in Africa, Asia, and the Americas—by any means necessary. A common strategy used by British imperialists was the Draconian rule of "divide-and-conquer." Historically, the modern form of imperialism during the colonial period of chattel slavery in America was predominantly triggered by economic factors rather than political or moral factors.

Case—A literary chunk of reality, designed to illumine issues, problems, and concerns through a dialogic process among individuals and social groups.

Chillin—A popular term used by many young African Americans to reflect a disposition of calmness, serenity under social pressure; relaxation, self-control or an unwillingness to show emotional reactions in the face of adversity.

Color bar—The prohibition against the full participation of a racial or ethnic group, identifiable by skin color, into the institutions or social life of the dominant group.

Contextual theology—A way of thinking about the *method* and the *content* of theology. Characteristic of this way of thinking is the importance given to alternative perspectives of discourse such as black theology, womanist theology, feminist theology, Latin American theology, Native American theology, etc.

Cultural racism—A systematic form of oppression of and domination as one race's culture is imposed on another; contributing to the devaluing and demoralizing of another's language, art forms, folkways, beliefs, and symbols of ultimate reality.

Cultural sexism—The gradual and subtle process by which a given culture imposes stereotyped sex roles on women and children in society; often contributing to low self-esteem and "feelings" of powerlessness. In America, this process of gender victimization is largely rooted in Eurocentric patterns of colonialism and laissez-faire capitalism, and maintained by a white male system of power and control.

Culture—Any pattern of learned behavior, pertaining to the individual or the ethnic group.

Cush—A term in the Bible referring to "the whole land of Ethiopia." The biblical scholar Charles Copher, in his book *Black Biblical Studies: An Anthology of Charles B. Copher*, writes the following: "Africa figures again in the earliest history in the account of the initial peopling of the earth as indicated in the Table of Nations (Genesis 10:6–10; 1 Chronicles 1:8–16) in which the eponymous ancestors of three African Nations or peoples (Cush/Ethiopia, Mizraim/Egypt, and Put [Phut]/Libya or Punt [Somaliland]) and their offspring are referred to."

The word "Ethiopia" and/or Cush, along with cognates, occurs fifty-eight times in the King James version of the Old Testament—Ethiopia thirty-nine times; Cush (untranslated), with cognates, nineteen times; and Put (Phut), identified as either Libya or Punt, occurs some seven times (See pp. 132–135).

Customary morality—The behavior of an individual or social group living in conformity with the prevailing social values and norms of a given group.

Ebonics—A controversial term coined by Robert L. Williams, a noted educator, to describe a process of communication peculiar to the historical experiences, values, morals, and cultural rituals of African American people. Therefore, "Ebonics" is a language. At the practical level, Williams believes that the goal of Ebonics is to enable students to better understand and master standard English, by taking them from where they are in language skills. At the conceptual level, Ebonics may be defined as the "linguistic and paralinguistic features which on a concentric continuum represent the communicative competence of the West African, Caribbean and United States slave descendants of African origin. It includes the various idioms, patois, argots, ideolects and social dialects of black people," say

Robert Williams and his colleague Ernie Smith. (See *Ebonics: The True Language of Black Folks*, Robert L. Williams, ed., St. Louis, Missouri: Robert L. Williams and Associates, Inc., 1975).

Epistemology—Theory of knowledge: one of the main branches of philosophy. Epistemologists raise central questions for reflection: e.g., what is the difference between knowledge and belief? What is worth knowing? How are knowledge claims justified?

Eschatology—In Christian theology, it refers literally to the "doctrine of the last things."

Ethical relativism—The ethical stance that there is no one correct view of things. Ethical relativists argue that sociotheological views vary among individual people, ethnic groups, and cultures ("cultural relativism"); and that there is no absolute standard for deciding who is right or what is wrong.

Ethics—It can be defined as *God-Walk*; ethics is the critical study of morality and ethnic behavior, in the light of certain prevailing principles of justice, love, equality, and freedom in human society. For the moral agent, ethics means the capacity to engage in the process of decision making: of discerning, choosing, and acting for the good of self and others; it is behavior according to reason.

Ethnic—Human collectivity based on a common origin, language, customs or social views.

Ethnic consciousness—A positive outlook which holds one's own group or value system to be a reference point for moral decision making and action.

Ethnicity— A critical concept referring to any social group and the prevailing values, sentiments, and beliefs of such a group: racial, ethnic, cultural, religious, etc.

Ethnocentrism—The term originated by W. G. Sumner to denote a pattern of thinking where most people use their own way of life as a standard for judging others; it also indicates the belief that one's race, culture, religion, or society is superior to all others.

Ethnogenic—Having to do with the ethnos; or pertaining to the origin and development of ethnic groups in human society.

Eudaemonia—(Greek:"living well"). In Aristotelian ethics, the view that the happy life is the good life. This word might also be taken to mean "happiness" particularly the complex and long-lasting kind of happiness implicit in the corpus of Aristotelian philosophy.

Extended family—A basic elemental unit of traditional African society and culture; the practice of a normative belief system which binds the individual in loyalty to a strict adherence to such a norm. For example, the Swahili word *Ujamaa* reflects the spirit of the extended family concept.

Feminist—An advocate for the full rights of women. (Feminists can be male as well as female.)

Foreign-born—Residing outside one's own place or country of birth.

Gangsta rap—Used to refer to any person, event, behavior or speech pattern that represents a rejection of the dominant culture and mainstream society's standards (See Gene Smitherman's book, *Black Talk*).

Institutional racism—A pattern of institutional privileges and benefits ascribed to a particular race, at the expense of other races or ethnic groups. Institutional expressions of racism may be conscious or unconscious, but the result tends to be the same in the U.S. work force: a denial of equal access and opportunities in a wide range of institutional settings—based on race, sex, color, class, nationality, religion, disability or sexual orientation. Because institutional racism in the U.S.A. is essentially based on power, the popular slogan "black racism" or "reverse racism" is largely a myth. Like all people, people of color can be prejudiced, but in America, they cannot be "racist" because they lack real control of institutional power to impose their will on the "white majority."

Kente-clothes—A certain fabric pattern of African origin usually worn by blacks or other people on celebrative occasions to highlight the achievements and contributions of people of African descent. The garment itself is imported from West Africa and represents solidarity and loyalty to religiocultural values and artistic icons in various African traditions.

Koinonos—A New Testament Greek work meaning "partner or companion," related to the verb *koinoneo* (to be a friend or a companion, or to share with others).

Minority group—A group regarded as different from the larger group of which it is a part in race, ethnicity or nationality, religion, or sex.

Moral responsibility—A philosophical stance which assumes that each individual is responsible for his or her own actions and dreams. Such a stance on the part of the agent underscores the poetic dictum I learned in grade school: "No one saves us but ourselves; no one can and no one may: we ourselves must walk the path; teachers merely show the way."

Morality—Behavior according to custom.

Mores—Folkways considered conducive to the welfare of society which, through general observance, develop into rules and laws governing actions of humankind.

Multiculturalism—A progressive school of thought which advocates respect for, and toleration of, cultural differences among people who do not share the same ethnic or religious background. Mutuality and cross-cultural affirmation in the search for a moral common ground are key watchwords in the multiculturalism movement in U.S. education and public theology. In social theory, multiculturalism rejects the notion of the white Anglo-Saxon Protestant as being the normative thread in the fabric of American life. In the same manner, its advocates also reject, for instance, the racist assumption that blacks and other minorities are less successful and more disadvantaged primarily because of a "lack of ambition," "laziness," or failure to take advantage of opportunities in the U.S.

Nigga—A provocative term used to reflect a variety of meanings, events, attitudes, implicitly or explicitly disclosed in the value system of American culture; e.g., it may refer to the fearless and rebellious "In-ya-face-individual" or the classic "docile Uncle Tom," popularized by racist movie tycoons to exploit people of color in the mass media.

Nommo—A philosophical concept used in the Afrocentric system of rational discourse by Asante and other Afrocentrists to unmask the biases and to resist the dominant ideology of Eurocentrism. Thus the concept of "nommo" refers to the generative and creative power of the spoken word.

Nubians—People of Negroid features or who possess distinctive physical features or shades of complexion and skin color deemed to be of the Negroid type and ancestry.

Pluralism—A concept that advocates the existence and preservation within a nation or society of groups distinctive in origin, cultural patterns or religion.

Praxis—Literally means "to do" or "accepted practice and custom," often used by Marx to signal the union of theory and practice.

Predilection—Personal preference, such as for one individual or for one culture, one skin color and/or one language as opposed to another.

Race or sex prejudice—Usually involves positive attitudes toward one's own race or sex and negative attitudes toward other races, and to the other sex. People belonging to any race or sex can be prejudiced.

Rapper—A term referring to a person engaged in the rhetoric of provocative black speech; one acquainted with a musical style of discourse, bleeding together both reality and fiction in response to the conditions of black suffering and rage in white America. Originally, the term "rap" referred more to a romantic style of speech designed to win over another person's love either in a sexual or platonic sense.

Sell-out brother—A derogatory phrase sometimes used to describe an African American who abandons the essential principles of black moral struggle, (e.g., unity, equal justice, faith, freedom, self-giving love, family solidarity, etc.), for the sake of personal gain or mere profit from white society.

Subculture—Ethnic, regional, economic or social group exhibiting characteristic patterns of behavior sufficient to distinguish it from others within a society.

Suffrage—The right or privilege of voting; franchise.

Theology—May be defined as "God-talk."

Velvetized racism—A critical concept in social theory differentiating a psychological form of racism that is largely unconscious or morally neutral, in the white individual who regards himself or herself as fundamentally a "good person." A typical scenario may be: "Oh no, I'm not prejudiced because my best friend is black (or Latino, Asian, etc.)," Concretely, what is distinctive and most disturbing about this form of racism is its capacity for self-deception and pretension. Hence it is like *velvet*, i.e., rationalistically "smooth" and self-serving. *Velvetized racists* have an inclination seemingly toward over-intellectualism. Many become "experts" on the problem of race or ethnicity; therefore, some hide their own ethnic sentiments, deep feelings, and bigotry behind the banners of philosophical liberalism, church dogmatics, or liberation theology in the Third World. I first coined this phrase in an essay entitled "Reflections on Cultural Racism: The Theoretical Task of the Black Ethicist," in *The Journal of the Interdenominational Theological Center* (Fall 1975).

Womanist—An advocate of the full rights and freedom of women and children of color; also men and "elders" of color.

Xenophobia—Hatred of foreigners or fear of strangers.